The Matrix Organization Reloaded

**Recent Titles in
Creating Corporate Cultures**

How Healthy Is Your Organization? The Leader's Guide to Curing
Corporate Diseases and Promoting Joyful Cultures
Imre Lövey and Manohar S. Nadkarni with Eszter Erdélyi

The Matrix Organization Reloaded

ADVENTURES IN TEAM AND PROJECT MANAGEMENT

Marvin R. Gottlieb

Creating Corporate Cultures
Fred Massarik, Series Editor

Westport, Connecticut
London

Library of Congress Cataloging-in-Publication Data

Gottlieb, Marvin R.
The matrix organization reloaded : adventures in team and project management /
    Marvin R. Gottlieb.
       p. cm. — (Creating corporate cultures, ISSN: 1935–6560)
    Includes bibliographical references and index.
ISBN 978–0–275–99133–3 (alk. paper)
1. Matrix organization. 2. Project management. 3. Corporate culture. 4. Teams in the
workplace. I. Title.
HD58.5.G68 2007
658.4'022—dc22   2007016134

British Library Cataloguing in Publication Data is available.

Library of Congress Catalog Card Number: 2007016134
ISBN-13: 978–0–275–99133–3
ISBN-10: 0–275–99133–4
ISSN: 1935–6560

First published in 2007

Praeger Publishers, 88 Post Road West, Westport, CT 06881
An imprint of Greenwood Publishing Group, Inc.
www.praeger.com

Printed in the United States of America

10 9 8 7 6 5 4 3 2 1

For
Aaron, Courtney, Payton, and Parker

Contents

Tables and Figures

Series Foreword

Culture is everywhere! Its study is not, for example, a narrow specialty confined to anthropology. Nor is it a specialty for those who seek to "change corporate culture," as proposed by many a consultant.

No one owns the word or concept *culture*. Indeed, it has numerous facets and complex ways of manifesting its impact on people and institutions. Nor is it defined exclusively by any one category of activity, such as language, ritual, housing, literature, or modes of dress, or by whatever is considered to be "good behavior," as in, "I met this really cultured person at a party last night...."

So what then is culture? In spite of the elaborate definitions and the extensive writings, there is no cut-and-dried single definition that serves all purposes. This series, Creating Corporate Cultures, takes a broad view of the subject. However one may seek the false security of one definition to fit all, it is our view that it is best to be eclectic and broad-gauge, exploring insights from many disciplinary viewpoints—including but not confined to anthropology, psychology, sociology, management, philosophy, and organizational development, among others—and as viewed from the vantage points of executives, consultants, academics, and hands-on people at work. Thus, this series regards culture not as a "silo," but as a field of many interacting forces, as a stream of human activities involving ideas, behaviors, norms, and manifestations of many kinds in which everyone is enmeshed day by day. Complexity rules!

One view of culture proposes that "it's just the way we do things around here." And as such this may be a reasonable starting point for getting at corporate cultures in action. It does not tell us however what things should be looked at and what "around here" really means. We will find that many authors focus on different "things" and bound their areas of interest "around here" in varied ways. We leave the specifics to the authors contributing to the series.

One aspect is clear: Cultures involve norms and values, and they usually have quite long durations in time. Sudden change is possible but rare. Mostly, cultures do not change overnight, and they manifest some measure of resistance to change. It does no good to simply yell at somebody, "Go change your culture!" This must be evident, if you consider the multiplicity of forces that act on people, especially when norms and values are taken into account. But as cultures *do* change, we know that this change can be purposefully facilitated by the people involved.

With this in mind, the series does not propose any quick fix. We hope, however, that each volume will constitute a substantial basis for thought and for action, helping along in creative culture change—in management, consulting, teaching, and improving the quality of the human condition at work.

ABOUT THIS BOOK

In our present world of organizations that is neither linear nor readily predictable, no wonder that it's time to "reload the matrix." While the idea of the matrix organization is not new of course, Marvin Gottlieb in *The Matrix Organization Reloaded: Adventures in Team and Project Management* provides a timely and deeply probing redevelopment of what this form of working together in complex systems can and cannot accomplish, as "bottom line" matrix emerges as a continuing important element in our complex global environment.

Gottlieb appropriately connects the matrix to the nature of corporate culture. Indeed, the matrix is not a "gimmick" but rather integral to how people work together as we have gone beyond the never-really-simple "make it/sell it/have people buy it" viewpoint. In this context, the author considers the evolving matrix and its challenges. He positions his contribution well within existing experience and with the pitfalls that need to be overcome to help the matrix function effectively. He considers "The Changing Face of Leadership" (Chapter 6) and "The Project Manager as Leader" (Chapter 7) and proposes sensible approaches for "Making the Matrix Work" (Chapter 10). Finally, he provides a practical tool, the RASIC, addressing issues of responsibility, approval, support, informing, and consulting, as well as a well-conceived and useful "Team Performance Inventory."

It is our hope that Gottlieb's effort will assist operating managers and those who study contrasting organization forms in facing rapid change, something inevitably present in today's complex world of work.

Fred Massarik, Series Editor

Preface

Writing a book on matrix management is like speaking out loud about "the elephant in the room." Like the elephant, almost everyone, when questioned, agrees that it is here, but there is a collective reluctance to talk about it. Many will go to extreme lengths to acknowledge that something is going on, but they will try to call it by another name. Perhaps no other organizational form has created the amount of ill will that the first launch of matrix management in 1970s and 1980s left in its wake.

But these are different times; the economics are different; the workforce is different; the whole world is different. Like the craftsman who tosses aside a strange shaped tool only to discover at some point in the building process that it was the perfect shape to accomplish an otherwise impossible task, many managers today are beginning to bring the matrix out of the shadows of the toolbox and are experimenting with its potential.

Writing about the matrix is elusive, as is any existing research that post dates 1980. To be sure, there are some fine examinations of both positive and negative applications of matrix management that carry more recent dates, and I have attempted to give them a fair hearing.

The key player in the matrix—the project manager—has received a great deal of attention during this same period. Much of the writing about project management is theoretical and complex, and focuses on process and metrics that many people charged with the responsibility of managing a project find difficult to apply in the real world.

More recently, some working project managers have been refocusing their attention and their writing on the people rather than the process. This is the point of view of this book. The success of any organizational design or any project ultimately rests with the people who have to live with the outcomes.

Employing an effective matrix structure begins with an understanding of the culture within which it must reside. Those managers who will succeed are the ones who are sensitive to the potential havoc that change brings to an organization, and will provide the necessary leadership, communication, and support to enable the people to adapt and realign themselves with the new reality.

Acknowledgments

I would like to acknowledge the extraordinary assistance that Bonnie Minkus, a scholar in her own right, has provided in conducting the research for this book, and the preparation of the manuscript. Her insights into multicultural issues were very useful in framing the material around globalization and cultural intelligence.

I am also grateful to all of the managers at various levels who took time to share their past and present matrix management experiences with me, so that real examples could be incorporated in the theoretical discussions as well as in the suggestions for practical application.

Introduction

THE MATRIX AND CORPORATE CULTURE

Since this book is part of a series on corporate culture, it seems fitting that we begin our discussion with the relationship between matrix management and the cultural climate where it tries to thrive.

The fact that culture exists as part of the total organizational phenomenon is no longer debated. Anyone who has changed jobs even within the same industry has experienced palpable difference in the climate and expectations of the separate organizations. We come to know these differences through the symbols, rituals, stories, and myths that exist within the cultural landscape. In the broadest sense, human beings create cultures out of a need for the feeling of control of their own actions and destinies.

As people we also strive to differentiate ourselves from others while providing a vehicle for establishing meaningful relationships. A culture provides structure and stability by helping us define who we are and how we should act with one another. When we are part of a culture we become interdependent with other members of that culture. Our ability to survive depends on successfully coordinating our activities with the activities of others. At the same time, all cultures exert influence over the behaviors of their members. The mechanisms of control in a culture are sometimes overt, but the most important control mechanisms tend to be covert and unobtrusive. Members are persuaded to accept the values of the culture and to act in ways that are consistent with the needs of that culture.

All cultures have subcultures within them. One needs only a quick look at current American society to see the manifestations of clashes between subcultures. Often the values of these subcultures come into conflict with the values of the broader culture itself. Within the broader culture people gather together to meet specific objectives, such as worship, commerce, or social activity. These groups develop unique characteristics and become organizations. All organizations are subcultures. Like the larger culture they share, they exhibit an incredible stability and a high resistance to change. It is against this backdrop of stability and resistance to change that a complex and, perhaps, revolutionary form of organizational structure, which we call matrix management, has tried to establish a foothold.

It is probably no coincidence that management training in the 1980s focused on corporate culture as a major topic at the same time that matrix management initiatives were trying to gain their foothold. Today a whole community of practice has been built around "change management" which, rightly understood, is an attempt to introduce changes into the organization in such a way as to be acceptable to the existing culture. Some organizations adapt more easily than others, and, as a result, have had more success with new forms like matrix management. One of the factors that could be dictating success or failure in this regard may be the view that top management takes toward the organization's culture.

All of the attention on organizational culture has in some ways created an overly simplified view of how organizational culture works. Charles Conrad (1994) in his book, *Strategic Organizational Communication*, presents a view of organizational culture and how different managers perceive it, which I support.[1] Conrad proposes a very powerful semantic difference in the way organizational culture is viewed by those whose job it is to nurture it. At one extreme there are managers and scholars who view culture as something organizations "have." From this perspective, culture becomes another element of the organization in the same way that organizations have equipment, buildings, health insurance programs, and other elements required to run the business. The culture is defined as shared assumptions, values, beliefs, language, symbols, and meaning systems that are an integral part of the organization. When the cultures are strong, employees throughout the organization at all levels share the same goals, have the same kind of feelings about the organization, and interpret the culture in the same way. Top managers in this view of culture can mold the culture strategically by persuasively communicating the core values of the organization to all of its employees and providing tangible and intangible rewards to employees who comply with the prescribed values.[2]

This perspective has been very attractive to organizational leaders because it suggests that they are the key in making organizations succeed. The underlying premise is that the culture is malleable and by applying some relatively simple tools they can improve their control over the employees' behaviors. After being introduced in the 1980s, the "organizations have cultures" point of view rapidly became dominant among managers and scholars alike. Viewed in this context, it is easy to see how top managers came to believe that they could implement the complex procedures associated with matrix management by promising significant short-term increases in competitiveness and profitability.

By expressing matrix management as a cultural value, it was assumed that all ranks of the organization would fall into line. While the voices of the critics of this approach were drowned out in a business climate that was trying to embrace the Peters and Waterman approach to "excellence," they were pointing out that advocates of the organizations have culture perspectives were never able to demonstrate that those factors that were selected and applied to create positive outcomes actually worked. There were further observations that over a ten-year period the firms selected by Peters and Waterman as exemplars of excellence were not any more effective or profitable than a randomly selected group of major American organizations.[3] There was also little evidence to indicate that lower level employees in so-called "excellence" firms actually shared the values and beliefs of upper management.

Because of the promise for major short-term, bottom-line benefits and the fact that planned cultural change is a lengthy, difficult, and unpredictable process, many managers who implemented culture change programs like matrix management found that the promised returns were not quickly forthcoming. When they realized that the "quick fix" approach wasn't going to work, they abandoned the program. Viewing organizational culture as something tangible, which can be consciously created and handed down by upper management, overestimates the ease of changing an organization's culture and the unpredictability of efforts to manage cultural change.

An alternate view presents culture as something that organizations "are." From this perspective we begin to see organizational cultures as intangible. They grow out of and are sustained by shared meanings that people assign to their surroundings. The glue that holds them together is the variety of formal and informal communication networks that exist side by side. They do not yield easily to persuasive strategies presented by upper management. As in the broader sense, members of a culture have unique ways of looking at and explaining the actions that are taking place around them. Members of a culture come to share in a worldview that differs from other cultures. The communication that takes place in an organizational culture helps people learn who they are and what is expected of them by members of that culture. It is through acting and communicating in appropriate and predictable ways that they make other members of the same culture feel comfortable with them.

Cultures have history; while slow to change, they continue to develop and adapt over time. However, even if major changes take place over time, much of the organization's history, many of its rituals, and even some of its artifacts remain stable touchstones for those who would identify the core cultural values that they represent. Anyone who spends a reasonable amount of time in an organizational corporate culture comes to understand the basic tenets of that culture. However, the "buy-in" to a culture is not universal.

Some employees immerse themselves totally in the cultural values, while others demonstrate a wide range of participation and belief ranging from selective acceptance to the cynical wholesale rejection of the cultural values as manipulative.

The organization itself may have subcultures that in some cases differ widely from each other in terms of adherence to the perceived core values of the organization. Even if the "organizations have cultures" and "organizations are cultures" represent opposite ends of the continuum, it is still apparent that corporate culture is a complex and powerful actor in the face of any prescribed change. Managers who perceived matrix management as a simple and direct way of addressing serious emerging business issues did not take this complexity into account. As a result, many potentially effective organizational initiatives were defeated by forces in the culture that would not readily adapt simply because they were ordered to do so. In the same way that politicians like to say, "All politics are local," those who promote change should probably say, "All change is personal." For this reason, any initiatives that neglect to account for the relationship side of change while focusing on the substantive side will most likely fail.

WHY LEARN ABOUT MATRIX MANAGEMENT?

We begin this book with a question, why should we learn about matrix management? This question is particularly appropriate for me since I had the opportunity to work as an organizational development consultant during the 1980s for several forward thinking organizations that implemented matrix management strategies. As well intentioned as these efforts were, for the most part, the results were not positive. In fact, in some cases, the experiment with matrix management bordered on disaster. Not only did productivity suffer, but also the heightened conflict that arose from the initiative had a negative impact on morale and can be pointed to as the basis for some very costly organizational mistakes.

Having observed much of this activity first hand, I must admit that I was a strong detractor of matrix management. Perhaps one of the most telling signs that I was not alone is the fact that no relatively serious writing on the subject has appeared in any publication since the 1980s. Most of the serious theoretical work focusing on matrix structures occurred in the 1960s and 1970s. So, I come back to the question, why should we learn about matrix management?

Without being overly facetious, matrix forms in organizations are like Freddy Kruger, the troublesome antagonist that simply won't die. In spite of themselves, most organizations today are in the process of morphing into matrix systems, randomly and without any formal preparation or support on how to manage this process effectively. There are many reasons for this, but primary among them are the demands of the marketplace, the continuous need for quick response, and the quest for innovation to provide differentiating products and services. Traditional organizational structures simply cannot respond rapidly enough to these demands. Manifestations of these matrix forms surface as "high-performance teams," "cross-functional teams," and other substructures of organizations that seek to align various points of view across traditional barriers.

As part of the process for writing this book, I had the opportunity to speak with many managers at various levels, in different types of organizations. Nearly all these managers had some sense of what a matrix system was and had a keen awareness that matrices existed in places in their own organizations. At the same time, not one of the managers with whom I spoke was able to confirm that any formalized orientation, training, or other support was being provided to ensure that the matrix was successful. Even some of the earliest matrix management theorists talked about the need for support mechanisms in order for the matrix to be successful.

Effective management of a matrix organization calls for the use of behavioral skills and structural mechanisms in ways that contrast sharply with those of traditional organizations. This web of relationships as described by John Mee has become even more complex with the growth of organizations organically, through acquisition, and as global entities, which not only provide fuel for matrix systems but complicate them because of their virtual nature.[4]

We need to learn about matrix systems because they are here and they are growing in complexity with every turn of the wheel. The dynamic pressures that a matrix system places on the organization provide opportunities for both conflict and redundancies in the way the organization operates. Later in this book, we will go into a discussion of the various types of matrix forms that can be incorporated. However, as part of the introduction, suffice it to say that all matrix forms have the potential for producing the same kind of conflict.

The underlying premise of the matrix is that authority at some level must be shared between two or more individuals. Whenever a matrix is introduced into an existing organization, functional managers mostly stay in their functional areas. As a result, many perceive this as a loss of authority to the project manager who holds domain over project activities that are in some cases operational as well as executive. Functional managers can come to feel that their involvement in a matrix system is limited to maintaining departmental resources. Project managers, on their part, feel unduly restricted by functional managers' control over departmental resources. As a result, the potential for conflict arises in which both parties try to enforce their will. If this condition is recognized and there is a well-understood methodology for facilitating agreement between these divergent points of view, these conflicts can actually result in higher quality decisions. However, without proper facilitation, they can spiral into mutual distrust and the conflict interferes with the effective functioning of the organization as a whole.

Managers need to learn about matrix management because it coexists with them in the environment where they need to be effective. It is important to understand that at every level of management there are strategies, techniques, and tools that can be learned and applied in such a way as to harness the power of the matrix to build effectiveness, creativity, and innovation into the organizational process.

This book is written for C-level executives, regional and department managers, project managers, and team leaders. Anyone charged with the responsibility for getting results through the use of cross-functional or other specialized teams whether on site or virtual needs to understand both the power and the pitfalls of the matrix. In addition, university classrooms that focus on organizational communication or business processes should spend some reasonable time acquainting our future business leaders with the realities of matrix management.

There are three primary objectives that this book tries to achieve. First, for those unfamiliar with the matrix despite already living with it, it is hoped that reading this book will familiarize those individuals with the characteristics and demands that matrix management puts on organizational leaders. Second, there is a hope that learning about the matrix and its potential will inspire the reader to experiment with the effective deployment of matrix forms that suit his or her particular organization. Third, the book will provide a methodology for analyzing, employing, and managing the matrix for the benefit of the organization, the manager, and the people who need to work with it.

The book is divided into two main parts. Part I, *Understanding Matrix Management*, provides a theoretical background against which the concepts of matrix management are displayed. Current experimental and anecdotal evidence are discussed, and applications are made to specific cross-functional events encountered in organizational environments. The reader will learn something about how matrix management evolved and will examine some early examples of matrix applications. Both successes and failures will be examined and supported by excerpts from managers who lived the experience. Different types of matrices will be discussed both from a theoretical perspective and from an examination of practical applications of the matrix as an attempt to meet business challenges.

Part II, *Embracing the Matrix*, provides practical guidelines for managers and others studying matrix configurations to enable them to lead and function more effectively in the global cross-functional, multinational environment. The reader will walk through a process of analyzing his or her organizational structure with an eye toward where the matrix has begun to evolve and to assess how the dynamics of the matrix are affecting key aspects of the way the organization functions. Once having either discovered an existing matrix or made the decision to move the organization toward a matrix structure, managers at every level need to examine the type of leadership necessary to positively engage the organization in a change process that leads to a mature matrix.

The book examines the various components of matrix management including high-performance teams, the effect of multiculturalism on the process, the growing role of the project manager, and the type of accountability the matrix demands from both those who would lead and those who wish to function as effective team members.

Finally, the book moves beyond the borders of the organization and examines the potential of managing matrix forms outside the organization. The growth of strategic alliances is examined, and suggestions are made about how to develop high levels of cooperation that cross organizational boundaries. The reality of outsourcing has brought into focus the special needs of teams that have been created out of an alliance. It is the hope that upon completing this book, the reader will gain some new insights and carry away a powerful model for managing both local and global business issues.

PART I

Understanding Matrix Management

The first problem we encounter when trying to understand matrix management is sorting through various definitions of the process to arrive at a construct that is operationally sound. Anyone contemplating the "reloading" of a matrix structure in his or her organization needs to have a firm grasp of what matrix management is, what type of matrix might be most useful for his or her purposes, and what plan needs to be put in place for communicating what is exactly meant by matrix management in his or her specific organizational setting to all the affected parties.

Perhaps matrix management is best defined in the way its structure contrasts with functional and divisional forms. Most organizational structures use the concept of "departments" to align the workforce and other resources according to products or functions. Functional organizations are segmented by key functions. Responsibilities for production, marketing, and finance might be grouped into three respective divisions. Within each division activities would be departmentalized into subdepartments. For example, the marketing division might include sales, advertising, and promotion departments.

Functional organizational designs have been the most prominent and most dominant form of organizations for a protracted period. The chief advantage of functional organizations is that they usually achieve fairly efficient specialization of labor. As such, employees clearly understand their roles and responsibilities. Functional structures also reduce duplication of work since responsibilities are clearly defined on an organizational-wide basis. On the other hand, highly functional organizations struggle with problems of communication, tunnel vision, and slow response to changing external conditions.

Divisional organizations consist of semiautonomous units and profit centers based on activities or projects such as products, customers, or geography. Each division operates as a separate business. Each business may be responsible for a particular geographic area such as Eastern, Midwestern, Western, and European divisions. In another manifestation, the organization might create separate divisions for consumer, industrial, and institutional products. One benefit of product or project departmentalization is that it facilitates expansion. A new division can easily be added to focus on a new profit opportunity. In addition, accountability is increased because divisional performance can be measured more easily.

The divisional structure encourages decentralized decision-making. Managers with specific expertise are in a position to make key decisions in their area. The key problems of the divisional structure include the expenditure of money and resources in the duplication of effort in different departments and a lack of horizontal communication between the divisions. Divisional organizations also tend to develop a strong subculture within each division that inhibits the ability of the total organization to focus on the overall company goals.

The matrix structure represents an attempt to combine functional and product departmentalization. The objective is to simultaneously organize part of a company along product or project lines and another part of it around functional lines to get the advantages of both. Within a matrix, each of the product groups intersects with each of the functional groups, signifying a direct relationship between product teams and administrative divisions. Theoretically managers of project groups and managers of functional groups share some level of authority within the organization. For example, in a balanced matrix the authority would be equal. The structure also dictates that many employees report to at least two managers. Some matrix structures exist on a temporary or ad hoc basis. Various work configurations or teams are created to deal with a particular problem or project. Once the objectives are reached, the team disbands and the members are reassigned to other duties or projects.

More permanent matrix structures are aligned with product lines or processes. One example would be a brand manager who is responsible for overseeing the development and production of an ongoing product, but staff who work on the product may also contribute to other products from time to time. This permanent set-up creates accountability, coordination, and continuity for the product as a whole. At the same time, it enables the staff to generally have a direct supervisor who is not a product manager to be flexibly assigned where they are needed most. The biggest advantage of a matrix structure is that it facilitates rapid response to change in two or more environments. Matrix structures are flatter and more responsive than other types of structure because they permit more efficient exchanges of information. An additional result could be the more efficient use of resources than other structures.

With all the potential advantages, matrix structures have received much criticism for the several challenges created by the unique arrangement. As we will point out in later chapters, many workers may become disturbed by the lack of chain of command, and the resulting conflict between project and functional areas can be detrimental to organizational goals. Chapter 1 provides a brief history of matrix management and looks at some of the challenges through the eyes of people who have lived with it. The chapter also examines some of the prominent theories supporting matrix management. Chapter 2 discusses the workforce that is called upon to implement and live with the results of matrix management. It highlights several differences between today's workforce values and the values of the workforce of twenty to thirty years ago when the matrix was first introduced. Chapter 3 will look in more detail at how the matrix has evolved over time. In Chapter 4, the discussion turns to some of the challenges that deploying a matrix structure in your organization can bring.

CHAPTER 1

Evolving the Matrix

> In a lightning strike our secure top-down one-boss organization chart was pulverized, replaced by a "two-boss" structure configured more like a tic-tac-toe grid than a pyramid. Bewilderment prevailed—no one knew where to put the X's and O's on the new grid and the timing of the shocking announcement was perfect: Pearl Harbor Day, 1974.
>
> —Richard E. Anderson[1]

A BRIEF HISTORY OF CROSS-FUNCTIONAL COLLABORATION

It is very hard to pin down precisely when both the concept and the terminology associated with matrix management came into being. One school of thought suggests that the early forms of matrix management were inspired by a reaction to the human relations or "organic" models that grew out of Elton Mayo's experiments at the Hawthorne Electric Company. The organic models recognized the importance of human behavior and cultural influences in organizations. This was in contrast to the mechanistic school that stressed efficiency and production through control.

The organic models emphasized flexibility and adaptability through employee empowerment. Structurally the mechanistic organizations tended to be vertical or hierarchical with decisions flowing down through several channels. The organic models were comparatively flat or horizontal and had few managerial levels or centralized controls. The strength of the organic model was that it encouraged human creativity and motivation. The mechanistic models were generally insensitive to external influences such as shifting markets or consumer needs and discouraged innovation. Companies that employed organic management structures tended to be more responsive and creative. The downside of the organic models was a lack of efficiency and personal accountability.

In order to mitigate these difficulties, many companies during the mid-1900s began embracing a model that minimized the faults and maximized the benefits of different organic management structures. In 1947, General Chemicals employed a model in its engineering department that was later referred to as a matrix. In the early 1960s, a more formalized matrix method called "unit management" was implemented by a large number of U.S. hospitals. There is further discussion of the experiment with unit management later in this book.

One of the earliest attributions comes from a short article by John Mee in 1964 in a column written for *Business Horizons* magazine titled "Matrix Organization." Mee describes the matrix organizational design as having evolved from the flow of aerospace technology. Without saying why, he points to changing conditions that cause managers to create new relationships of established organizational concepts and principles. The matrix is described as a form that is meant to be flexible and adaptable in its use of resources and procedures to focus on project objectives.[2]

Even as early as 1964, Mee cites urgency for completion and a more efficient utilization of human talents as major factors for experimentation with the matrix. In these terms, the matrix organization is defined in relation to how it differs from the traditional divisional type of organization. He points out that in a divisional organization,

A division manager is responsible for total programs of work involving the products of his division. In a matrix organization, the divisional manager has the same responsibility, authority and accountability for results. Differences occur in the division of work performed as well as in the allocation of authority, responsibility and accountability for the completion of work projects.[3]

While this early definition of matrix management remains a pretty accurate description of today's matrix forms, matrix structures have been with us for centuries. One can argue that the Roman Legion was designed along matrix management lines. John W. Hunt (1998), a professor of organizational behavior at London Business School, writes in an article for the *Financial Times* that matrix structures are anything but new. He makes the point that any family can be described as a matrix because there are potentially two bosses, the mother and the father. He also asserts that government departments have been operating dual authority structures for more than a hundred years.[4]

The aerospace program in the United States is widely credited for giving credence to the matrix system. Feeling the pressure to close the "missile gap" drove the industry toward a more innovative way to utilize people. This strategy called for a two-boss matrix. One boss focused on technical excellence and owned the specialists, the other acted like a general contractor, used the specialists as needed, and steered the product program through the organization maze to the customer. For the aerospace industry this worked very well. In addition to the productivity benefits derived from the form, splitting the resources in this way actually reduced costs.

The expensive specialists could be allocated to multiple projects, thereby cutting down on high cost head count. Also, because the specialists worked out of functional home bases, they could be redeployed quickly to reconfigure organizational resources to meet new customer requirements without complaint.

At the project level, the experts who knew best what was needed were empowered to make decisions and process information at will. This alleviated any hierarchical bottlenecks caused by the necessity of channeling everything in an upward direction. Through horizontal interaction across the organization, work was allowed to proceed without intervention. Top managers found that the matrix structure freed them from the day-to-day firefighting across organizational lines and allowed them to concentrate on strategic issues.

Arguably, the matrix system worked very effectively for the aerospace industry. During that period several factors conspired to enhance the effectiveness of this design. Perhaps the primary reason was that the aerospace companies were responding to a single customer, such as the Air Force. Because of this, the production emphasis shifted to the completion of a specific work project, rather than managing the flow of work on production programs for a large volume of products. As projects were completed or abolished, they simply disappeared from the organization.

When the focus of an organization is on a specific product or project, it makes sense to provide a manager with the authority, responsibility, and accountability for the completion of that project. This includes the timing, cost, and quality issues spelled out in the project contract. Regardless of the functional associations of the project team members, priority is given to their work with the team, and any functional associations are secondary. In this way, the project team or suborganization is charged with both the responsibility and the accountability for the success of the goals and objectives.

It's important to note that in this successful model, the project manager is all-powerful. He or she has the authority to design and assign the work to the functional group members as well as to establish reporting relationships. The project manager also has authoritative input for reward, promotion, salary, and other incentives while the project is in process. When the project is completed or otherwise terminated, the functional personnel return to their departments for reassignment to other projects or for training to develop new skills.

In expressing his enthusiasm for this organizational form, Mee describes the American manager as possessing a proud record of ingenuity and creating new organization schemes to adapt to changing technological and economic requirements. "The matrix organization design is no exception. It permits a higher degree of specialization for human talents with maximum efficiency of operations."[5] Despite the enthusiasm, Mee expresses some concern for the adaptability of American organizations. He points out that unless managers and operating personnel are educated and trained to work with the matrix design, they will be frustrated, incur emotional disturbances, and lose motivation. "Working in an environment characterized by change as projects are started and completed is not as comfortable and secure as performing a continuing function in a more stabilized standardized workflow situation."[6] The accuracy of Mee's observations is uncanny, and they foretold the very pitfalls that matrix management experienced in its early days. These same admonitions are as relevant today as they were then.

One of the early problems in migrating the matrix structure to industries outside of aerospace was the attempt to turn the matrix into a bureaucracy. The fact is that matrix structures can range from the very simple to the extremely complex. A simple matrix program may consist of liaison roles that provide coordination across functional departments. At the other end of the spectrum are matrix programs that sequentially add a matrix director, a matrix department, and a horizontal hierarchy with authority rivaling the vertical-functional hierarchy existing in an organization. Driven by the need to increase response time and innovation in the product lines, many large organizations in the mid-1970s saw matrix management as a panacea and jumped in with both feet.

Richard E. Anderson (1994), a past employee of GE's (General Electric) major appliance division and the source of our quote at the head of this chapter, describes the introduction of matrix management at GE.[7] Although he says he did not realize it at the time, the dramatic changes in his organization were a reflection of other GE businesses as well as of other large corporations. GE had experienced success with this form in their aircraft business long before they applied it to the appliance business. The company's medical business also installed two-boss matrix management in the mid-1970s. The bandwagon was rolling; Dow Corning's worldwide matrix was widely discussed and written about. Xerox, Texas Instruments, TRW, and Citibank were in the process of experimenting with two-boss matrix management. Digital Equipment Corporation developed computers and other innovations in a free form matrix based on reporting to two bosses or sometimes more than two depending on the product development situation.

Anderson left the appliance business in 1977 and later determined that the power sharing that worked efficiently for missile projects did not transfer well to washers and dryers. The major appliance matrix developed stress cracks and failed a few years after it was formed. Among the other organizations engaged in the matrix experiment, Dow Corning's failed as well. People at various levels at Xerox referred to their matrix as the culprit behind their company's decline in the 1980s, and Digital pulled the plug on matrix management around the same time. By the mid-1980s, it was hard to find anyone to defend matrix management.

THE RISE OF TEAMS

As we look back on the history of matrix management, we might be left to wonder whether the matrix form ever really passed out of favor or simply changed its nomenclature. By the mid-1980s, the concept of "teams" had captured the corporate imagination. One widely heralded team application was the Ford Motor Company's "Team Taurus." The Team Taurus initiative consisted of a small group of full-time members from engineering and manufacturing, while the other functions such as purchasing, castings, and outside suppliers were matrixed to the group. Following this lead, Chrysler put together the Viper team, and many other large U.S. corporations were trumpeting stories about cost savings and shorter production times. Again, the emphasis was on integrating functions across the normally separated departments with an eye toward increasing the efficiency of the decision-making process and creating an environment where team members could build consensus and commitment.

It is probably best to view the successes of these programs in the context of their time, for, at the writing of this book, Ford Motor has just announced the demise of the Taurus line and is laying off one-quarter to one-half of its workforce. Further discussion about teams in context will appear later in the book; however, the fact that these efforts seem to have failed, at least for Ford and others in the long term, should not detract from the probability that at the time they were instituted, the teaming approach was a powerful and successful innovation.

In order to gain perspective on the essential differences between the world of aerospace and the large corporations who either experimented with or adopted the matrix wholeheartedly, it is necessary to contrast the differing corporate climates and cultures. Many of the large corporations that adopted both matrix and later team structures were positioned in the marketplace much differently than the aerospace industries. Several of these companies maintained market dominance for their products. Many companies could control their prices and raise them in conjunction with their competitors, and products enjoyed very long life cycles. NCR, for example, didn't change its cash register significantly for thirty years. Product innovations could be stacked up to not disturb a dominant design, then ruled out when a major model change finally replaced an aging product line. Breakthrough innovations were sought over the long term in centralized corporate research centers. This complacency created a long period of quality decline. Consumers tolerated shoddy products because worldwide comparison was unavailable.[8]

Even more innovation-focused companies like Reuters, where I consulted for a long period from the mid-1980s to early 1990s, were dominated by centralized bureaucratic control. Various innovative tracks were established, which theoretically were intended to function as high-performance teams, but in reality yielded to the fixed hierarchical structure of the main organization. While Reuters is a good example, it is by no means unique.

Those companies that commanded market share and enjoyed significant capital assets tolerated these independent units with their own functional goals.

In the case of Reuters, many of these efforts did yield significant innovations. However, many others were colossal and expensive failures. Sincere efforts were made in these individual corporate units to function as a team. However, in most cases, it was necessary to gain cooperation and resources from functional departments and units in order to accomplish the desired goals. The battle over controlling these resources was and continues to be one of the major pitfalls of the matrix.

The traditional functional units such as marketing, sales, administration, and IT displayed little interest or concern, and even less cooperation with each other. One of my roles as a consultant at Reuters was to facilitate the breaking down of some of these barriers. In one instance, during a software development project, I managed to get representatives from all of the necessary functional groups in a room at the same time to discuss the project. I was astounded to discover that this was the first time any of these individuals had been together in the same place. In fact, many only knew each other by name even though they were all fairly high up on the management chain.

Matrix management and cross-functional collaboration was mandated but not facilitated. Top management, having laid out the plan on paper, made the assumption that it would be carried out. They isolated themselves from the reality of what was actually happening and were ultimately swept from leadership. Even though the software project at Reuters was ultimately a success, it should come as no surprise that an organization with people who were embedded in a functional pattern for their whole career did not receive matrix management with open arms when it was suddenly thrust upon them.

By the mid-1990s in corporate America, a widespread cynicism developed around the notion of matrix management and project teams. One of the best expressions of this cynicism comes from Michael Schrage (1998) in an article for *Computer World*. Schrage, at the time a research associate at the MIT media lab and the author of *No More Teams!*, refers to the IT world's experience with matrix management and teams by asking the question, "Who really benefits in a matrix management structure?" Schrage's view is that the key beneficiaries and power brokers of matrix management are the top managers. Matrix structures and teaming, he suggests, guarantee that there will be overlapping lines of responsibility in reporting among groups that have different goals, incentives, and sensibilities. "In other words matrix management guarantees conflict." Because of this conflict, top managers must step in to resolve the very conflicts and disputes guaranteed by the organizational design. Rather than fostering cooperation and collaboration, matrix management foments heavy politicking to ensure that top management retains the power to distribute resources. He goes on to suggest that from the IT point of view, matrix management makes top management look fully engaged by making it so difficult for the IT and business managers who actually do the work to work better together.[9]

Not everyone engaged in the matrix management experience that spanned the forty years between 1960 and the turn of the century shares this level of cynicism. But the matrix as an organizational form has garnered widely mixed reviews, and most of them are negative. As such, what accounts for the tenacity of matrix management's components? Why do we see more of these elements reemerging and taking center stage in many of today's organizations? Perhaps there is something inherently correct in the matrix structure that continually reasserts itself. Add to that, the extraordinary conditions in today's economic environment and corporate culture appear to match better with matrix requirements.

Globalization, stiffer competition, and radically changing workforce values have significantly changed the way companies operate. Product cycles have shortened drastically, and the focus is on flat, lean, team-centered organizations, focused on business processes that by necessity cut horizontally across functions. There is a sense of urgency that pervades product development.

For many organizations, the adoption of matrix management in the early years was a response to the perceived success in the aerospace industry. One key difference between what happened in aerospace and the imitators that were looking for the same type of success was that the matrix in aerospace *evolved* from a necessity to respond to their key customer—the Department of Defense—that needed more direct involvement and faster turnaround on design and production than could be had with the traditional hierarchical functional forms. Many companies seeking the potential benefits from matrix forms *imposed* matrix management on an organization unprepared to absorb the change, and then failed to provide the level of support that would help ensure success.

Perhaps the opinion of those who feel that matrix management grew out of the human relations movement is correct. The early experiments were successful because the project teams enjoyed a high degree of autonomy and a significant relationship component with each other and the customer. The "cloned" matrix events that were imposed on traditional organizations ignored the relationship component and created a sterile environment in which a successful matrix could not grow.

In the next chapter, we will look at the workforce from both an historical perspective and contemporary manifestations. The success or failure of the matrix is inextricably connected to the people who have to live with it.

CHAPTER 2

The Workforce and Corporate Culture

Salaried workers at General Motors are bracing for cuts expected to come as early as today, according to U.S. reports.... [Spokesman] Robert Herta told AP the company won't respond to rumors, but he said GM has already announced plans to cut 7% of its U.S. salaried work force this year.

—Just-Auto.com[1]

It is difficult, if not impossible, to pick up a newspaper, magazine, or any other business-related media and not be confronted with at least one announcement about workers losing jobs or added concerns and burdens for those who remain employed. As this book is being written, U.S. government reports are documenting that new job creation has slowed, and the jobs that are available are at salary levels well below what workers were earning. There is also an escalating resistance on the part of older workers to retire. It appears that many "boomers" are electing to stay on the job.

One doesn't have to think back too far to conjure up pictures of an entirely different world. For today's workers, the world of the past is gone and has changed so radically as to be unrecognizable in present-day terms. And, lest we forget, this has happened very quickly. When matrix management burst on the scene some twenty-five years ago, it impacted a very different workforce.

There was a time—and, I reemphasize, not too long ago—when the major issue of discussion and debate at colleges and other places, where the future shapers of the world would meet and discuss issues, was what we were all going to do with the inevitable leisure time that we saw developing on the horizon. Some of you may recall having taken part in those debates. Shorter work days, four-day work weeks, and the like seemed to be the future, along with the accompanying benefits and social problems that were projected to arise within a leisure society. Some estimates suggested that by the turn of the century, we could have either a twenty-two-hour work week or a six-month work year or a standard retirement age of 38.[2]

THE COMMITMENT GAP

Having bought into this notion, hundreds of thousands of upwardly mobile workers in all categories, firmly convinced of a straight-line projection of leisure into the future, began to reshape their approaches to work and their concerns about self-fulfillment. They purchased second homes, boats, and other leisure-related toys in extraordinary amounts.

In essence, workers, and particularly managers, who felt that they were keeping their side of the bargain—going to college in ever-increasing numbers and trading off portions of their newly coveted personal freedom for corporate concerns—believed that they were in the driver's seat. They believed that unless they seriously screwed up, they would always have a job, and if one job didn't please them, they could readily find another.

They further believed that the organizations they worked for, since they made up the organic material of those organizations, would have to bend to suit their developing needs. In short, in the early 1980s, as the economy continued to grow, workers—and particularly educated workers—believed that they were in control of their destinies. They certainly did not envision a future that would reposition them as victims. One can readily see that with this as a backdrop, radical change in their work life was not high on most workers' wish list.

WORK AS A RIGHT, NOT A PRIVILEGE

In 1983, Daniel Yankelovich presented some extraordinary findings and conclusions about changes in the workforce in his book *New Rules: Searching for Self-Fulfillment in a World Turned Upside Down*. In many respects, Yankelovich foreshadowed the major cultural shift of the 1990s and beyond. When my colleague Lori Conkling and I studied the effect of massive downsizings on the workforce in the early 1990s, we also realized that once stable workforce values were undergoing a major paradigm shift. We documented these findings in our book, *Managing the Workplace Survivors: Organizational Downsizing and the Commitment Gap*.

While Yankelovich's perspectives were the result of a myriad of interwoven extrinsic and intrinsic factors—including a rapidly changing American (and world) economy, the civil rights and women's rights movements, and the post-Woodstock adoption of a wider range of choices, values, and life-styles—they all pointed to a radical change in the self-identity of the American worker. The fundamental value of "hard work pays off in the long run" was called into question.

[T]ens of millions of Americans have grown wary of demands for further sacrifices they believe may no longer be warranted. They want to modify the giving/getting compact in every one of its dimensions—family life, career, leisure, the meaning of success, relationships with other people, and relations with themselves...to the efficiency of technological society they wish to add joy of living. They seek to satisfy both the body and the spirit, which is asking a great deal from the human condition.[3]

Yankelovich saw people engaging in a new social ethic gradually taking shape. He called it an "ethic of commitment" to distinguish it from the traditional ethic of self-denial that underlies the old giving/getting compact, and also from the ethic of duty to self that grows out of a defective strategy for self-fulfillment.

In 1979, Yankelovich's company, Yankelovich, Skelly and White, set out to survey almost 3,000 Americans employed either full- or part-time in the United States. Yankelovich's methodology for culling the essence of these new rules included conducting several hundred life-history interviews and drawing on a number of large, previously published national surveys of the American workforce.

Yankelovich's findings were startlingly revealing of our personal values, due largely to these open-ended life-history interviews. People were asked to describe what self-fulfillment and success meant to them in the most personal sense of these terms. The people discussed their values, moral convictions, and life goals and contrasted their own personal feelings about success and self-fulfillment with how their parents felt about those matters and pursued them in their own lives. The respondents were also asked to recount the risks taken for the sake of success and self, and the risk each had chosen to shun.

Two significant statistical entities emerged from these studies: One of the larger changes we discovered in the research was a sharp drop in the number of college students who believe that "hard work always pays off." In the mid-sixties, 72 percent of college students subscribed to this view. By the early seventies its adherents had been almost cut in half—to 40 percent....In the decade between the late sixties and the late seventies the number of Americans who believe "hard work always pays off" fell from a 58 percent majority to a 43 percent minority.[4]

While not on the scale provided in the Yankelovich study, our own research with a fairly large sample of both managers and employees in financial services organizations concurred with these findings.

The research also revealed that one group of working Americans placed their personal self-fulfillment high above all other concerns about money, security, performing well, or working at a satisfying job. This group constituted about 17 percent of all working Americans (approximately seventeen million people at that time). They were younger than average, and more of them were professionals than among average Americans. When surveyed, fewer had married or owned their own homes than average Americans, and their politics leaned more toward the liberal than toward the conservative wings of the Democratic or Republican parties. They were also the best-educated of five groups, with more than half (51%) having received at least some college education. Also, their parents had much more college education than the rest of the working population (42% to 21%).

The most important phenomenon that emerges from these dynamic shifts in American values and attitudes continues to appear in the contemporary workplace. Yankelovich refers to this as the "commitment gap."

This phenomenon was a shock to the late baby boomers, and the next generation was more wary. As baby boomers move into retirement or semi-retirement, their places in management will be filled with the members of Generation X. Generation X, born between 1965 and 1979, is a much more pragmatic generation than their predecessors and will bring that strength to their management duties. They are likely to focus on improving processes inside the office and developing new and more efficient ways of conducting business. They are comfortable in delegating authority, promoting transparency in the office, and coming to decisions quickly. They are much more concerned with balancing work and personal lives than previous generations and are not afraid to change employers if they feel shortchanged. Because they are such a small generation, the most talented members among them, especially those with prior experience, will be in very high demand.

In order to understand some of the resistance to new organizational forms and the demands they made on workers with changing expectations, we have to understand the climate of tension and rebellion the young workers of the 1970s participated in. Nothing could have been further from the values of these self-fulfillment seekers than the class-conscious, hierarchical, authoritarian, adversarial attitudes that characterized the managerial outlook in many American industries at the time. Rebelling against the status quo, workers who were engaged in the search for self-fulfillment retaliated by holding back their commitment, if not their labor. They were struggling to revise the giving/getting compact in the workplace at a time when many organizations were instituting structures that appeared alien, and seemed to make additional demands on their time and energy. For them to give themselves unstintingly to the job, they demanded in return important psychological incentives as well as economic ones. These demands made them troublesome to work with—as a condition of their commitment, they were constantly demanding things for themselves.

From the organizational perspective, work is perceived as a privilege rather than a right. The single choice that is offered to today's workforce is to earn and re-earn, sometimes on a daily basis, the right to continue to be employed. The only other option—that is, to dive or be pushed over-board—is a terrifying prospect to a vast majority of essentially risk-averse people, who began their work lives with the assumption that they would be taken care of.

It is little wonder then that members of the baby boom generation (aged 40–59 in 2004) feel more overworked than employees in other generations. A new study by the Families and Work Institute, *Overwork in America: When the Way We Work Becomes Too Much*, takes a comprehensive look at working conditions and attitudes today. According to the study, boomers work longer hours on average, are more likely to desire fewer work hours, more frequently experience interruptions at work, more often have elder care responsibilities, and have higher average earnings (which indicates a higher level of respon-sibility on the job) than other groups of employees. While the study associates all of these factors with a feeling of being overworked, it also illustrates some of the resistances to implementing change that might bring even more work. Also, older workers are not known for their receptivity to new approaches that will turn their world upside down.

When the study compares boomers with other employees in other birth cohorts, the apparent difference between boomers and others in being overworked disappears. Thus, being overworked is a function of the kinds of jobs employees have, not their age or generation.[5]

RESISTANCE TO COMPLEXITY

Why is the experience of being overworked pertinent to matrix manage-ment? I would hypothesize that much of the perception of being overworked comes from dealing with the complexity and ambiguity that derive from the demands of the current business environment. The study by the Families and Work Institute shows how prevalent this feeling is based on 2004 data.

- Twenty-six percent of employees felt overworked *often* or *very often* in the last month;
- Twenty-seven percent were overwhelmed by how much work they had to do *often* or *very often* in the last month; and
- Twenty-nine percent *often* or *very often* didn't have the time to step back and process or reflect on the work they were doing during the last month.

The study also found that

- Forty-four percent of U.S. employees were overworked *often* or *very often* according to at least one of the measures, while only 29 percent say they *rarely* or *never* experienced being overworked. When employees who reported being overworked at least sometimes are added to the total, the proportion of employees who are overworked increases substantially.

The researchers found that the more overworked employees are

- More likely to make mistakes at work. Twenty percent of employees reporting high overwork levels say they make a lot of mistakes at work vs. none (0%) of those who experience low overwork levels.
- More likely to feel angry at their employers for expecting them to do so much. Thirty-nine percent of employees experiencing high overwork levels say they feel very angry toward their employers vs. only 1 percent of those who experience low overwork levels.
- More likely to resent coworkers who don't work as hard as they do. Thirty-four percent of employees who experience high overwork levels vs. only 12 percent of those experiencing low overwork levels say they *often* or *very often* resent their coworkers.

A well-functioning matrix culture requires collaboration, trust, and a willingness to share control over individual territory for the good of the collective. If the intent is to develop an effective matrix, these work-related and interpersonal issues need to be addressed prior to changing the organizational structure.

The overriding concerns in the recent past about a leisure-oriented society sound as a distant echo in the caverns of today's reality. The new workforce is an entity caught up in the flow of rapid and continuous transition—transition to what, we don't yet know. However, one thing is certain: the workforce of today, and what it will become in the future, is starkly different from either what it was or what was expected only a few years ago.

Today's workforce is grappling with a distorted perspective of time and its value as a personal commodity, due largely to the uncertainties of job security and economic growth. Rather than experiencing more leisure, those employees who are lucky enough to survive downsizing, restructuring, or reengineering are finding themselves putting in a marked increase of work time, partly due to the fact that they are now assuming two or three other jobs, which have been "rightsized" out of the corporation. Rather than being able to give their full attention to one job, many workers are finding themselves matrixed to two or more jobs.

Many of today's employees are also burning the midnight oil, due to their employer's shortsightedness that work is getting done only when an employee displays his or her undying commitment to the organization by pushing papers around the desk after 5 p.m., no matter what is actually being accomplished. Because many people focus mainly on *time worked* as the major predictor of being overworked, they overlook other aspects of the way we work that are, in fact, more significant predictors of being overworked than hours worked. Particularly important is lack of "focus"—or more precisely, the inability to focus on one's work because of constant interruptions and distractions as well as excessive multitasking required to keep up with all that has to be done on the job.

Obviously, the ability to multitask is very important to succeeding in today's economy. The point is simply that the way we work today may be asking some employees to multitask too much without providing the necessary support mechanisms to make it work. One reason that excessive multitasking has become standard fare in many jobs is that job pressure is on the rise. There is simply more work to do, often with less time and fewer people to do it. The matrix is coming into play without any conscious intention to deploy it. In addition, there is a wide perception that much of the work required in today's organizations is of low value. The study by the Families and Work Institute asked subjects to respond to the following question: "I spend a lot of time at work doing things that I think are a waste of time." Overall 29 percent of employees *strongly* or *somewhat* agree that they spend a lot of time doing things that are a waste of time. Importantly, those who agree are more likely to be highly overworked: 51 percent who feel they have to do a lot of low-value work are highly overworked vs. 25 percent who don't feel this way.

In the previous research, the Families and Work Institute's study identified a number of factors that are characteristic of an effective workplace—that is a workplace where both the employer and the employees fare better. This study found that employees who have jobs that provide them more opportunities to continue to learn, whose supervisors support them in succeeding on the job, who have the flexibility they need to manage their job and their personal and family life, and who have input into management decision-making are less likely to be overworked. This is true even when they work long hours and have very demanding jobs. This sounds very much like human relations thinking and could provide a basis for supporting the relationship side of initiating change.

CREATING CULTURAL SHIFT

The evidence seems to show that much cultural change can be affected in a positive way by top management. However, organizational leaders need to do more that rearrange the organizational chart. In 1984, Noel Tichy and David Ulrich, writing in the *Sloan Management Review*, saw "fat and flabby" U.S. companies engaged in a gradual decline in the increasingly competitive world economy. They called for a new brand of leadership to *transform* organizations and head them down new tracks. Further, they charged their leaders of the future with the responsibility of making major changes in the basic political and cultural systems of the organization. Much of what they had to say about the role of leadership maintains its validity today—with some modification. Tichy and Ulrich were tied to the basic hierarchical model. Although they used phrases like "lean and mean," they didn't foresee (or at least describe) the flat matrix structures that were emerging and continue to develop today. They placed their hopes on the CEO as the initiator and modeler of change. Their idol was Lee Iacocca. Discussing the effectiveness of Iacocca's turnaround at Chrysler, they point to his involvement on the "relationship" side of the issue.

This bailout came with a stigma, thus Mr. Iacocca's job was to change the company's cultural values from a loser's to a winner's feeling. Still, he realized that employees were not going to be winners unless they could, in cultural norms, be more efficient and innovative than their competitors. The molding and shaping of the new culture was clearly and visibly led by Mr. Iacocca, who not only used internal communication as a vehicle to signal change but also used his own personal appearance in Chrysler ads to reinforce these changes.[6]

In addition to transformational leaders, the hard realities of a faltering economy during that period had a major effect on cultural change in organizations. A subsequent wave of change in the form of increased workforce diversity also influenced cultural changes. While Tichy's and Ulrich's views do not reflect today's reality, the basic model they suggested for managing change has considerable application. Separating the major targets for change into organizational dynamics and individual dynamics, they constructed a model that took into account trigger events, forces resistant to change, potential interventions, and the results of such interventions.[7]

Using their model as a springboard, the model in Figure 2.1 was created to demonstrate the process of moving those caught up in a change initiative through various stages toward what we might call "realignment." In the initial phase, there is a "change driving event." This can be stimulated by

Figure 2.1
Change Management Model

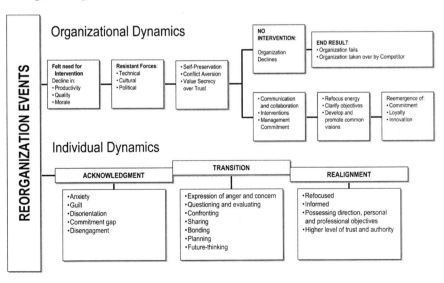

economic conditions, a change in the market, new technologies, a take over, profitability, a need for operational improvement, and other factors that require attention. The initiation of a major change often causes a decline in productivity, quality, and morale. The employees experience anxiety and disorientation leading to a potential commitment gap.

As with all change, forces within the organization move to maintain the status quo. Here, the model borrows Tichy's and Ulrich's resistance categories: technical, cultural, and political.[8]

Technical resistances include habit and inertia, fear of the unknown or the loss of predictability, unwillingness or inability to adapt to new technology, and focus on the investment already made in old approaches (sunk costs).

The culture of the organization creates selective perception and tunnel vision. It inhibits the ability to employ innovation as a means for adapting to change. Also, there is a comfort level already attained with the current culture that is hard to give up. There is a security in the past and a general feeling that if we just wait this out, we'll get back to the "good old days."

Political coalitions draw tighter lines around their boundaries. Tendencies for territoriality become overt competition for dwindling resources. Managers are reluctant to rescind decisions or abandon objectives they have only recently made. Everyone becomes more acutely aware of their perception within the organization, and much time is spent "covering backsides."

On the organizational side, these resistances lead to a preoccupation with self-preservation, conflict to protect territory, and the valuing of secrecy over trust. The individuals express these feelings through cynicism, anger, sabotage, and the withholding of effort. If something isn't done at this stage, the initiative, and even the organization, will, most likely, decline.

In the midst of all these forces interacting, there is one factor that remains within the control of managers at every level; that is, how much and in what form they are willing to communicate. Managers who succeed in maintaining high levels of quality and productivity during periods of change are those who proactively deal with the feelings and information needs of their subordinates. In the absence of solid information, rumors fill the vacuum. The enemy of any effective change strategy is ambiguity.

To be successful, any interventions developed to support matrix initiatives should have three parts: an acknowledgment phase, a transition phase, and a realignment phase. Managers and subordinates must face squarely that they are living in a new order; that, while the future is uncertain, there is no going back to the past. The anxiety they feel is more about the uncertainty of their own future than the "good old days." Managers must believe and project that there is a future and that what the future is will become clear in time. They must be self-disclosing about their own anxieties but also provide a model of commitment that others can see and emulate. This is a far cry from simply drawing lines on an organization chart and expecting people to adapt quickly and quietly.

THE ILLUSION AND REALITY OF CHANGE

Despite all of the media focus on organizational change, if we were to take a snapshot of the attitudes, values, beliefs, and lifestyles of a cross-section of today's workers, how are they really being affected? Despite the enormous changes between the workplace of the 1950s and the high-technology, global work environment of today, the same motivators matter most to us as people and workers, those factors such as intrinsic personal satisfaction and gaining the attention of our supervisors and colleagues. While these satisfiers, such as making a good income and having control over work content and schedule, are important, long-term commitment and motivation still emanate from within, from individual internal needs and values—here, we have the most potential for success.

We cannot minimize the importance of providing a highly participative working environment, where people perform meaningful and interesting work, where they feel they are significantly contributing toward a higher goal, where they can achieve a healthy balance between their work and their personal and family life, and where career development and growth are valued and encouraged. Making these values an integral part of matrix management will go a long way toward assuring success.

The implications for almost immediately positive impact and change in the workplace are highly apparent. By focusing on the quality of day-to-day supervisory practices and activities, functional and project managers can build and maintain a more committed workforce. In fact, most managers today seem to be taking concrete steps in that direction. Certainly, the employee–supervisor relationship is a key linchpin in the implementation of organizational change.

Unless organizational leaders pay attention to the relationship side of managing change, the culture will ultimately defeat their best efforts. Daniel Yankelovich and John Immerwahr[9] have drawn conclusions based on the distinction between motivating factors and satisfying factors, discussed in the last chapter. They claim that it helps to explain the somewhat ambivalent feelings that American jobholders have about their managers. Many people like and respect their managers. On the basis of their surveys, nearly seven out of ten workers, when asked, said that their managers were more interested in getting the job done than just bossing people around. Six out of ten said that morale in their place of work was good or excellent.

But the positive feelings that Americans have about their jobs and managers change dramatically when the focus shifts from satisfaction to productiveness. Three-quarters of the workforce (75%) believe that the inability of managers to motivate the workforce is a key reason why people are working less than they could.

A focus on job satisfaction, in other words, does not necessarily enhance work ethic values. If managers want to capitalize on the considerable human potential that already exists in the workforce, they must focus on the key motivators that will realign workers in a productive way, and not confuse those motivators with satisfiers which, although nice to have, do not necessarily yield more productivity.

MATRIX TEAMS HAVE SPECIAL NEEDS

Project management has evolved to the point where processes and performance metrics are highly sophisticated. However, communication and relationship factors are the primary source of problems. My firm, The Communication Project, Inc. (TCPI), consults for a major national laboratory. In 2004 and 2005, TCPI was contracted to consult on the development and maintenance of high-performance teams charged with the responsibility of conducting laboratory-directed research and development. As part of this process, a climate survey was conducted at the beginning of the project and at the end. Individual interviews were also conducted with several members of the team, and other materials were collected as a follow-up to the survey.

The survey was administered to fourteen members of the research team. The questions were approved and/or modified with the input of a selected group of subject matter experts from the lab to ensure that they were relevant to the work setting at the laboratory in general and the research team in specific.

A distillation from the debates about what constitutes effective teams and work groups points to the conclusion that most well-working high-performance teams seem to exhibit a set of nine common characteristics. They are

- Clear objectives and agreed goals
- Openness and confrontation
- Participation and trust
- Cooperation and conflict
- Workable procedures
- Leadership
- Benchmarking and review
- Personal development
- Good intergroup relations

The results from the survey indicated that there were some areas where clarification, open communication, and collaboration could have a significant impact on the overall performance and work-life quality of the research team. Two categories stand out as having significant agreement among the group: *workable procedures* and *clear objectives and agreed goals*. Other categories, while not quite as high, show considerable agreement as well. While the characteristics are fairly descriptive in their own terms, below are definitions for the two top-ranked categories.

WORKABLE PROCEDURES

High-performance teams place a premium on results but also realize that sound working methods and decision-making lead to achievement of objectives. Clarifying objectives is essential, as it can prevent all the misunderstandings and defensive arguments that result from some members not knowing what is happening. For decision-making, good groups develop the ability to collect information quickly and then discuss the alternatives openly. They then become committed to their decisions and ensure that action ensues quickly.

CLEAR OBJECTIVES AND AGREED GOALS

No group of people is likely to be effective unless there is a collective understanding of what needs to be achieved, but having clear objectives and agreed goals is more than just knowing the intended outcomes.

People are most likely to be committed to objectives if they also feel some identity with and ownership for them. Even where the objectives are understood and agreed upon, a gap often exists between organizational and personal objectives. One of the chief indicators of effective realignment is that this gap has been narrowed as much as possible. Effective high-performance teams recognize both personal and group needs.

Since a relatively small group was polled, an item analysis was done to determine if there was agreement on individual questions in the survey across the nine categories. The picture that emerged was a group that could benefit from some established guidelines, clarification of authority, clear definition of tasks, delegated responsibility, and the opportunity to establish ownership of the mission. Because the group was de facto a matrix unit, application of established matrix management methodologies would help alleviate much of the stress that is eroding productivity and morale.

On the basis of this research, several recommendations were made.

- The matrix that has evolved could be more effective in supporting the mission. The team has evolved as a matrix management system that most closely resembles a Project Matrix. A Project Matrix has three key components: (1) Team members move between functional departments and projects and retain membership within both units for the duration of the project; (2) During their tenure with the project team, members focus most or all of their energy on team goals and objectives; (3) While assigned to a project, team members are under the direction and management of the project manager. The current matrix has a high degree of ambiguity as to focus, responsibility, reporting relationships, and evaluation. Clarification of roles and responsibilities and a reconceptualization of the team vs. functional unit obligations will provide a significant boost to the operating efficiency and effectiveness of the team.

- Knowledge/skills are needed to support the matrix. For a matrix management system to operate optimally, the team members and their functional managers have to have a basic understanding of how the matrix works, their role in it, and how to use existing tools for managing tasks and responsibilities, deliverables, timelines, and success metrics.

- Opportunities and methods are needed to enhance teaming, creativity, and innovation. Currently, most group activity is conducted as a "work group" rather than as a "team." Team members are carving out pieces of the project that fit within their comfort zone and working independently. High-performance cross-functional teams need structured opportunities to do actual work as a group rather than just meeting to report on individual progress.
- Widen the focus of staff to target customer needs. The climate survey and subsequent materials submitted by team members point to a preponderance of "why" questions. Most answers to "why" questions are derived from an understanding of who the client is and what the client's needs are.
- Nurture entrepreneurial thinking and team spirit within the group. Team spirit and entrepreneurial thinking generally grow out of a success with the previous elements. Successful teams thrive on openness, trust, mutual respect, and belief in the capabilities of other team members.

ACTION STEPS

Several action steps were taken to address the issues of the team.

1. The current team membership was evaluated for commitment, focus, and competencies (technical and interpersonal) for moving forward.
2. Some personnel changes were made, including replacement of the project manager. Functional managers with staff working on the team was pressed by upper management to agree that reporting relationships, evaluation of those members, and time commitments are controlled by the project manager; the team commitment must take precedence over functional commitment.
3. Some coaching was provided for the new project manager, including group process dynamics needed to motivate team performance and facilitation skills to meet the special needs of the matrix management system.

At the end of the project, the team was surveyed again. Most of the issues were resolved, and the team rated their performance significantly higher. The change in project management had a major effect on the outcome. The new project manager adopted a much more collaborative style both within and outside the team. As a result, the relationship between the team, the stakeholders, and the functional managers was greatly improved. This resulted in more clarity of the mission and a lessening of the conflict associated with the competition for resources.

This chapter has attempted to shed some light on the primary role of the workforce: The people who are most affected by the introduction of a change like matrix management. Changes in both the expectations and the realities of working in today's organizations have created ambivalence toward the organization that was once seen as secure if not nurturing. Where there is ambiguity, there is mistrust, and collaboration falters. When the organization places emphasis on communication, relationship guiding, and inclusiveness, it allows the people to share in the excitement and promise of change and stimulates cooperation and innovation.

Chapter 3 will turn our attention to the basic philosophies of matrix management and examine some of the hybrids that have emerged out of necessity or by accident rather than design.

Structuring the Matrix

Effective management of a matrix organization calls for the use of behavioral skills and structural mechanisms in ways that contrast sharply with those of traditional forms of organizations. Nevertheless, most matrix organizations arise out of these traditional forms.

—Harvey F. Kolodny[1]

OVERVIEW OF MATRIX MANAGEMENT THEORY

The complexity of the matrix structure is rendered more accessible by studying the backdrop of theoretical literature on the subject. While it is not the purpose of this book to either postulate or repeat existing matrix management theory, it will be useful for the practitioner to have a working knowledge of the various points of view about matrix management presented over the last forty years. As was pointed out in the Introduction, most of the serious theoretical work focusing on matrix management was done in the early years, from the late 1960s to the end of the 1980s. Except for an article here and there, very little has been written about this important organizational cultural form.

One of the challenges of highlighting the theoretical underpinnings of matrix management is that a pure matrix form is highly elusive. Matrix processes can exist in a variety of structural arrangements and accompanied behaviors. Several of the early theorists (e.g., Galbraith 1971, Kolodny 1979) viewed the matrix form as transitional. The matrix phenomenon was seen as representative of various stages in an historical progression from one organizational form to another. Kolodny (1979) points out that where an organization was with regard to the adoption of matrix management depended on the information processing demands of its environment. Those organizations that depended primarily on rules, hierarchy, plans, and direct contact with one another internally were classified by Kolodny as conventional, functional product forms. Those organizations that employed information processing designs that incorporated liaisons, task forces, and teams tended toward the matrix end of the continuum.[2]

C.K. Prahalad (1976) supports the view of the matrix as a transitional form. He provides a case study about how a multinational corporation swings from area domination through matrix structure to product domination as power shifts in the organization.[3] Pradip Khandwalla (1977) goes a step further by asserting that the matrix structure is not a pure organizational form. He categorizes it as a hybrid, product-function form, "a combination of the principle of specialized departments with the principles of self-sufficient, more or less autonomous units and divisions."[4]

While accepting these views as a legitimate perspective, Kolodny supports the notion that an organization travels a road from a hierarchical design to matrix design. He points out that not all organizations follow the road completely to the really full matrix organization at the end. Some stop along the way because they have found the appropriate form for their situation.[5] This developmental process suggests that matrix programs that move incrementally through various stages toward a pure matrix enjoy greater survival prospects than fully implemented matrix programs.

MATRIX DRIVERS

Whether the matrix is instituted by design or happenstance, certain environmental factors are almost always present that result in matrix activity. Some of the earliest examples provided by Galbraith and others, as well as current examples, contain the same components that I have observed over time. It generally happens like this. The organization experiences an inability to respond in timely fashion to problems arising in its environment. This can be variations or innovations required in the product lines, the rise of new competition, or an increase of complexity in product–market relationships. Contemporary examples also add the complexity created by technological changes that alter fundamental ways of doing business and threaten critical products with obsolescence.

Assuming the company is large enough, these factors will be experienced in many different areas of the organization. It soon becomes clear that some type of collaboration is going to be required in order to meet the challenge. The entrenched vertically structured hierarchy cannot cope with these collaboration requirements, and the organization responds by decentralizing around specific tasks. These tasks are assigned to a specific coordinator or project manager. Under the best of conditions, these responses are customer driven. The organization begins to acknowledge that explicit structural actions need to be taken to ensure that the management of its projects and the sensitivity to the clients are not left in the hands of traditional functional managers, whose priority is their specialist orientation.

At this stage, project managers ideally acquire and assemble relevant resources, plan, organize, and control the tasks and activities. They are provided with both the responsibility and the authority for decision-making, since the project level is where knowledge relevant to the decision issues can be brought together and where the activities and results can be monitored. In this way, as the organization as a whole becomes more decentralized, individual projects experience a higher level of centralized control.

Of course, the issue is never that simple. Project teams are rarely large enough to command all of the resources necessary to meet their goals. As a project moves through various stages, requirements for resources change and the need to share resources becomes a clear requirement of the situation. Again, under the best of circumstances, the necessary resources are provided through the decentralized support that comes from a variety of functional units within the organization as well as from outside consultants, subcontractors, suppliers, customers, and any other relevant sources needed for the project.

A successful project-centered organization steps outside of conventional bureaucratic assumptions. Four factors come into play: (1) using horizontal coordination as well as vertical, (2) providing project managers as alternative authority figures to those with hierarchical position power, (3) focusing on tasks that are of limited duration and not conducive to bureaucratic strengths of increasing efficiency through repetition and working down the learning curve, and (4) delegating decisions downward to autonomous units rather than constantly bucking them up the hierarchy.[6]

In a perfect world, this project organization stage unlocks the strangle hold of the bureaucracy. The organization as a whole moves toward a new reality. A period of learning takes place, and new behaviors and communication patterns come into play. It's at this stage that the organization elects either to remain in the project mode, and thereby solidify that structure as the new organizational form, or to continue on the path toward full matrix management.

A project-centered organization differs from a full matrix organization in that the focus is on completing temporary tasks in a fixed amount of time for set costs and according to a specified set of performance standards. The manifestations of these tendencies can be seen in more recent times in the rise of quality control mechanisms like ISO 9000 and Six Sigma. One of the primary goals of the project manager is to put himself or herself out of business. In a full matrix organization, the role of project manager is elevated to a higher level. The intent is that the processes and behaviors applied to the project form will be continuous for an entire line of business, or, in some cases, for the overall business itself.

The project manager then becomes a "matrix manager," responsible for the ongoing business, its profit and loss, its success or failure, and its future potential. In a mature matrix culture, the balance of power clearly shifts from

Table 3.1
Matrix Structures

General Matrix Orientation	Functional	Balanced	Project
Project manager's level of authority	Very limited—depends on relationship influence	At same level as functional managers	Maximum authority over project design, staffing, budget, and client interface
Organization personnel with full-time project assignment	None—all functional personnel assigned to the project are temporary	Varies with the perceived need for project work, but accounts for 50% of assignments	Most personnel are involved with project teams and return to the functional area until needed for a new project
Project manager's commitment to project work	Part-time and temporary	Full-time—either managing a product or shifting projects as the need arises	Full-time—responsible for a major portion of the company's business
Project manager titles	Coordinator, Project Lead, Facilitator	Project Manager, Team Leader, Project Officer	General Manager, Program Manager
Project administrative support	Part-time and temporary	Some full-time supplemented with part-time as needed	Full-time and dedicated to the work of the project

This chart shows the basic matrix structures and characteristics associated with the project manager.

the functional manager toward the project or matrix manager. Participation in teams becomes a rule rather than an exception for most organizational members, and multi-team membership becomes a way of life. Some of the distinguishing factors of the mature matrix organization are explained below.

Response to the Environment

New functional groups develop as the need arises. The organization grows and acquires and divests itself of different organizational units and recombines its resources in a variety of ways.

Boundary Crossing

Project/matrix managers are free to contract for services outside of the organization that could potentially be provided in-house. At the same time, functional units are free to sell their services outside of the organization.

In this way, matrix management becomes a systems model of organization because of its ability to capitalize on overlapping resources within the organization and open access to and from the environment.

Collaboration and Influence Behaviors

The matrix provides a framework that requires employees to combine and recombine in a variety of teams, task forces, projects, programs, product groupings, and functions. Matrix members learn the collaborative skills needed to function in an ever-interacting environment. Conflict resolution skills also become heightened because each team is multidisciplinary and differences in orientation must be managed.

Increasingly in today's matrix form, multicultural elements add to the complexity of team configurations. Good interpersonal and communication skills are a key component because the nature of team relationships calls for clear and unambiguous communication, and there is little time to resolve problems centering on emotional and personality differences. Group process skills are paramount as the necessity for consensus decision-making replaces individual- and authority-based decisions.

The Types of Decisions Drive the Balance of Power

Both functional- and team-based activities are important to the organization, and the balance between them will shift according to various conditions in the environment. When economic times are tight, power shifts in favor of those dealing directly with the products and services of the organization since they are more concerned with profit and loss and short-term performance. If the economy is strong, emphasis is likely to shift to the functional areas where new approaches, technologies, and other developments will allow future projects and programs to respond with more innovation.

The Use of Strategic Anticipation

In a traditional hierarchical organization, functional managers tend to be reactive. In a matrix setting, functional managers need to learn to anticipate the needs of project and matrix managers. This is particularly true in a pure matrix, since project managers are free to buy their needed services outside. This causes functional managers to develop their own internal value propositions and look for ways to be responsive to their internal marketplace.

As an organization gravitates toward a matrix structure, some functional departments will find themselves struggling for relevance. Training departments are a good example. In addition to the prevailing view in many organizations that training is a cost that is easily trimmed in tight economic times, training managers have generally done a poor job of connecting what they can offer to the core objectives of the business and responding rapidly as need occurs. As the matrix develops, project and product leaders who have training and development needs often find it necessary to contract for these services outside of the organization.

THE CHANGING ENVIRONMENT AND COMMUNICATION

When organizational environments are stable, demands for communication are relatively small, and problems that arise are common and repetitive. Because they have precedence, there are tried-and-true solutions ready to apply. Without the ever-changing pressures from the environment, traditional organizations can cope quite well with the limited amount of uncertainty they face.

Coinciding with the interest by researchers in the matrix management form, other researchers were more specifically looking at the way a stable or unstable environment made demands on the communication systems in organizations. Paul Lawrence and Jay Lorsch (1967) studied the communication systems of successful firms with stable environments and compared them with successful firms in unstable environments.[7] They found that organizations in rapidly changing environments are more effective when they work in communication structures that allow a free open and rapid flow of information. This is contrary to the restrictive, formal, and slow chain of command type of information flow in traditional organizations. They argue that open communication structures more readily receive information about sudden environmental shifts and disseminate that information throughout the organization more quickly. In an open system, employees who have relevant information or expertise can be involved in deliberations about how the organization is able to best respond.

There are many variables that account for a rapidly changing environment. For example, sources of raw materials are not particularly stable and predictable. Petroleum continues to be a good example of this. A new variable in the current economy is the industrialization of China and India, which has placed immense pressure on raw materials such as steel and concrete. Another variable is ongoing changes in production technology. Perhaps the most fickle is customer preference and market demands. One example often cited involves plastic products. A warehouse full of hula hoops in 1985 represented a total loss; however, if you had sold and destroyed them in 1986, how would you have reacted when the demand was back in 1989? Nearly a decade later, hula hoops were once again a saleable item.

Part of the problem of selling matrix forms to the organization as a whole is that pressures from the environment do not affect every member of an organization in the same way or to the same degree. Some employees find themselves very close to the source of uncertainty. A manager concerned with acquiring the necessary raw materials is going to be more highly affected by a changing environment than a manager concerned with packaging and delivering finished products. A marketing manager will be much more concerned with trends and shifts in individual taste than a distribution manager who has established outlets for products when they are ready to be put on the shelf. Perhaps some of these factors can account for marketing missteps from stable traditional companies like Coca-Cola, bringing at great expense "New Coke" to a tepid and unreceptive market.

The coffee industry presents us with another interesting example. The industry developed a strategy based on the assumption that as people mature, they turn away from childhood preferences to more adult pursuits; the coffee industry geared up production to service the rapidly growing population whom they believed would be switching their beverage preference to coffee. In fact, just the opposite is true. In 2001, *American Demographics* reported that the coffee market was undergoing a crisis of demographic proportions. The study pointed out that coffee drinking in the United States has been on the decline for decades as many consumers, especially younger ones, have continued their romance with soda and added bottles of water, sports drinks, and other new beverages. While Starbucks helped to buck the overall coffee market decline with the "coffee house craze" of the 1990s, the availability of coffee to go actually served to undercut the market for coffee at home. Only 21 percent of 18–24-year olds drinks one cup of coffee or more at home daily. Despite the obvious environmental factors, coffee makers continue to spend the bulk of their ad dollars on hooking middle-aged consumers. Per capita consumption of coffee dropped to about 17 gallons in 2000, down from 36 gallons in 1970, while soft drink consumption grew to 55 gallons over the same period.[8]

Should we believe that these problems would be mitigated if an effectively functioning matrix were in place? The deployment of a matrix structure does not guarantee success in dealing with a turbulent environment. However, if implemented carefully and effectively, it does open up opportunities for the organization to have access to the kind of information that would lead to better decision-making.

ORGANIZATIONAL CULTURE AND THE MATRIX

As we discussed in Chapter 2, one of the key environmental factors influencing the matrix is the radical change in the workforce. It is interesting, if not coincidental, that the rise of interest in matrix management parallels the changes in the workforce since World War II. Factors such as increased education and altered expectations have continued to evolve from the mid-twentieth century to present day. In the heyday of traditional organizations, only a small proportion of the workers had completed even eight years of formal education. Today, only a tiny proportion has not done so. Most workers today have finished high school, and a large percentage of them have college degrees. As early as 1983, one-quarter of employed Americans held bachelor's degrees, the first time in history that such a high proportion of the workforce had college education.[9]

It stands to reason that highly educated workers expect to have jobs that use their creative talents and training and provide them with opportunities to participate in decision-making. From mid-century to much of the 1980s, the key issue for managing this new workforce was keeping them motivated, since a paycheck in and of itself no longer did the job. The old compact between worker and company was still in force. Most workers, who did not make exceptional blunders, could still anticipate long-term if not lifelong employment with a particular company and a good retirement package at the end.

Today's workforce is grappling with a distorted perspective of time and its value as a personal commodity. Largely, as a result of the uncertainty of job security and economic globalization, many of today's workers have already experienced the dislocation of downsizing, restructuring, or reengineering, and the "leaner-meaner" organizations they work for are making stronger demands on their employees than ever before. Many of the managers interviewed as part of the preparation for this book claim an affinity for the principles of matrix management; however, they feel that it was difficult to become an effective participant in the process because they were being pulled in too many directions at the same time. This factor feeds elements of resistance in the culture, not only toward changing structure, but also toward change in general.

CONTINGENCY THEORIES AND THE MATRIX

Matrix management in various stages of maturity is directly related to an organization's attempt to adapt to pressures from other systems both internally and externally. These pressures cause organizations to adopt modes of behavior and communication that allow rapid dissemination of information and quick adaptive decision-making. By decentralizing organizational structures and allowing participatory decision-making, organizations can adapt rapidly to the changing environment.

Perhaps the best theoretical underpinnings for matrix management are contingency theories. Contingency theory argues that an effective organizational response is "contingent" on a number of factors. Later in this book, we will discuss how contingent factors affect the behavior of project and team leaders. It is sufficient to point out here that the contingencies driving matrix forms require sophisticated and flexible leadership.

- They have to be individual contributors in a significant way.
- They have to be effective communicators.
- They have to balance toughness and compassion.
- They have to be accessible without being overwhelmed.

- They have to be energetic and driving without bringing too much stress to others.
- They need to appear courageous, committed, and consistent to those who report to them, and those to whom they report.[10]

Despite the fact that not a great deal of focus is being placed on matrix management per se, contingency theories seem to dominate modern organizational theory and organizational communication theory. Based as they are on the complex interrelationships included in systems theory, contingency models indicate that individual satisfaction, performance, and organizational effectiveness depend more on adapting to the situational, technological, environmental, and personal variables than on the application on any single approach. Contingency theory fits well with matrix forms because it concerns itself with the processes through which organizations use communication to manage ambiguities, uncertainties, and complexities.

MATRIX CONFIGURATIONS

As complex as it may be, the matrix structure is a very fragile entity. While no specific organizational form can be guaranteed to succeed at all times, some organizational forms have a better chance of working than others, particularly if they are aligned to meet the perceived needs of the organization. If factors in the environment have determined that the continued success of an organization depends on effective project work, then matrix management meets a number of well-defined needs.

Perhaps the most pressing need is for a structure that can handle the great complexity of a multidisciplinary effort. If the need for cross-functional collaboration is really apparent and the organization must become more project driven, then the matrix is a viable solution. Matrix systems consist of a complex collision of both organizational and human factors; as such, they will not automatically work. There are certainly a number of things that can go wrong, and many have already been discussed and will continue to be discussed in later chapters. One of the most prominent reasons for the failure of matrix management is foot-dragging or downright sabotage on the part of functional management, often in concert with lower level supervisors. If the matrix is to work, everyone must be a believer and every effort must be expended to make it work. I strongly believe that the matrix can and will work, and, when it works, it will result in an outstanding accomplishment. However, it only takes one uncooperative element in the organization to make the whole initiative fail.

Because of the many factors that drive matrix responses and the variety of responses available, matrix forms are difficult to pin down. If one accepts the evolutionary theory of matrix development, it has to be assumed that the form is in continuous change. This may reflect the true state of matrix management in a given organization. However, a practitioner preparing to introduce the matrix or make an existing matrix more effective needs more definitive information. He or she needs to ask questions like the given below:

- Do matrix processes already exist within the organization?
- If they do exist, are these matrix processes effective?
- What can be done to support the positive aspects of the matrix and mitigate the problems it may be causing?
- If matrix forms exist within the organization, are they taking the same form throughout the organization?
- How can the organization effectively expand matrix processes to parts of the organization not currently engaged?

A recent article by Sy and D'Annunzio (2001) identifies three matrix forms that have distinct characteristics: functional matrix, balanced matrix, and project matrix.[11] These three categories have become embedded in almost any discussion of matrix management and stem from its earliest theorists.

Functional Matrix

In the functional matrix, employees remain primarily attached to their functional departments. When the need arises from environmental pressures, the organization institutes procedures to help facilitate cross-functional collaboration. In a functional matrix, the project management role is limited to coordinating the efforts of the functional group. The functional managers retain the primary responsibility for the design and completion of the project objectives.

Balanced Matrix

The balanced matrix is what most people think of as the classic model. We have referred to it earlier on as the "two-boss" model where employees are officially members of two organization dimensions inside the organization. They retain their full membership in a functional department, but find it necessary to balance their energies between the functional department and the specialized projects to which they have been assigned. In a balanced matrix, project managers take on more of a leadership role in defining what needs to be accomplished and the time limits. The functional managers hold sway over the actual staffing of the projects and much of the resources the project team will need to accomplish their objectives.

Project Matrix

In a project matrix, employees retain an association with functional departments but have the freedom to move between their functional objectives and various projects almost at will. The organization as a whole takes on a project management overlook. Project managers acquire primary control over the direction, the project, and the resources needed to accomplish the objectives. In a project matrix, functional managers take on a consultative or advisory role—provide support for the team responsible for carrying out plans and controls established by the project managers.

In Chapter 5, we will use this three-part construct as a springboard to the observation of how matrices may already be functioning in your organization. While few, if any, organizations are purely one category or other, the characteristics associated with each category provide benchmarks for analyzing an organizational structure, to determine what type of matrix is most evident in the organization. Making this determination is step one in any scheme to enhance matrix management.

CHAPTER 4

The Challenges of the Matrix

> Shortly after announcing her retirement, the PMO director described a strange personal experience. She was working at her computer when a wild, crazy feeling came over her. She almost broke the suffocating silence surrounding her with a scream. Later that night, a similar feeling overtook her on her commute home, nearly causing an accident. Speaking with a therapist later that week, she mentioned these curious occurrences. After some reflection, the therapist responded, "You've been feeling happiness." After some reflection, she accepted this as truth. She'd touched ground. She had forgotten what happiness even felt like! Happiness, you see, wasn't one of the success metrics she had been focusing on in her 38-year career trying to formally control projects.
>
> —David A. Schmaltz[1]

In this chapter, we begin to look at some of the reasons behind the successes or failures of the matrix form. Even without experiencing matrix management first hand, it is easy to see where obstacles will inevitably arise. First and most obvious is that the introduction of matrix management is a significant change from an existing vertical-functional authority toward a hybrid function-by-project organization. Despite contrary assertions, vertical organizations rarely promote teamwork in the real sense. The word "team" itself becomes associated with a more common form of work group, which has little, if any, authority or responsibility for its own destiny.

Matrix structures always look good on paper. They appear to satisfy several operating and strategic needs. They create opportunities for resource sharing, structure profit center integrating for large projects, satisfy customer requirements, address competitive pressures, and serve specific market segments.

Because of the enthusiasm that this potential solution creates, management either overlooks the strength of the entrenchment, and siloed functional units within an organization, or makes an even greater error by assuming that these barriers can be managed by directive. Many top managers that I have worked with over the years were shocked to discover the low level of acceptance and compliance expressed by middle managers and employees charged with carrying out matrix management directives.

All organizational design contains many of the same elements. These include structure, management systems and process, formal and informal interpersonal relationships and networks, and motivational patterns. Each organization is going to exhibit its own unique characteristics within the parameters of this design. These organizational characteristics emerge as the "culture." The case that organizational cultures exist is not one that needs to be made here nor should it be necessary to argue the power that organizational culture asserts on the individuals in the culture. Despite their uniqueness, all organizational cultures have one thing in common. As subcultures of the broader culture around them, they reflect the primary values of that broader culture.

One of the factors that makes it difficult for matrix processes to gain acceptance is what some theorists call hegemony. The concept of hegemony rests on the observation that most societies are hierarchical in many ways. When we internalize the taken-for-granted assumptions of our culture, we internalize its hierarchical relationships and come to see them as normal and natural. Therefore, any attempts to break down these hierarchical arrangements are often met with heavy resistance. There are many examples of how hegemony plays out in corporate culture, but our focus here is on the role it plays in the acceptance or rejection of matrix forms. Change at this level causes those involved to question their basic assumptions. The imposition of matrix management or any other potential structure perceived as outside of the norm forces members of the organization to ask questions about their most basic beliefs, about what is natural and normal as cultural choices, rather than absolute truths. This is difficult because it asks people to question assumptions that make their world seem stable and predictable.

Moving away from the traditional organizational forms is particularly difficult for many organizational leaders. Management style and organizational form are inextricably related. Significant changes like those associated with matrix management require major shifts in style for many executives. The most receptive executives will be those who have good interpersonal skills, are comfortable with delegating, and enjoy the intellectual challenge of a healthy debate. They favor flatter, more participative designs and feel less threatened about sharing the decision process. On the other hand, executives who have a high need for control, are detail oriented, and demonstrate a strong ability to organize prefer hierarchical closely managed configurations.

Management style, particularly in senior managers, is difficult to change. Much of the failure to effect change lies with the corporate executives themselves. They may begin with the best intentions to design and align the workforce within a corporate strategy that will gain a competitive advantage for the company as a whole or for a SBU (strategic business unit); however, they tend to view the organization mechanistically rather than holistically. As such, they rearrange organizational components, such as reward systems or measures, and ignore the changes in other components caused by the realignment. Management experience in a traditional organization teaches people to focus more on refining the parts rather than the whole. As we discussed earlier in this book, the "copycat" matrix management implementations that attempted to replicate other company's designs failed largely because the executives made the mistake of assuming that an organizational design that works well for a market leader in their industry or a similar industry will work for them as well.

Discussing the advantages of flexible organizational forms, Miles Overholt (1997) captures the essence of how an executive needs to view his or her organization as a prelude to initiating change.

Flexible organization executives are more innovative, preferring organization configurations based on several factors. They examine their company's market needs, the host country's culture, the competitors and the nature of the industry, and the core competencies. They assess how different organizational designs can provide a competitive advantage in different scenarios. In short, they manage organizational design as they manage any other aspect of their organizations, as a strategic initiative that needs to be revisited regularly to ensure that it is contributing maximum value to the corporations' performance.[2]

It is almost certain that many of you reading this book, have yourselves, at one time or another, expressed negative feelings in the face of a new initiative. You have probably even discussed with colleagues that "given enough time the new initiative will go away and everyone can get back to business as usual." The power of cultural norms is evident in this little scenario, because without support, the new initiative, matrix management or some other, will probably fail and thereby support the original premise that it would in fact fail. This point is raised here because the implementation of a matrix structure or the support of a self-emerging matrix must be addressed on the cultural level. Later, we will get into some of the specifics of how to address these cultural issues. However, as we look at some of the successes and failures of matrix management, we can see how this underlying principle comes into play.

FACTORS ASSOCIATED WITH ADOPTING A MATRIX STRUCTURE

An interesting study done about fourteen years ago by Lawton Burns and Douglas Wholey (1993) examines some of the reasons why organizations adopt or abandon matrix structures. While their study was rigorous and well defined, it focused exclusively on a type of matrix management called unit management, which came into use in hospitals beginning in the 1960s. Despite the limited scope of the study, many of the findings and conclusions are useful for the examination of matrix structures in other organizational types. Their objective in doing the research on the adoption of matrix management was to improve the understanding of factors favoring structures that promote product innovation and quality management.[3]

Unit management was selected as the object of the study because it exhibits several of the matrix management characteristics and was widely adopted by hospitals as a means to promote the coordination and integration of functional department personnel. Unit management programs place administrators in inpatient units to act as liaisons and coordinators of all functional department employees working in the units, such as head and staff nurses, housekeepers, dietary aids, technicians, and social workers. The idea was to provide these unit managers with decision-making responsibility, including developing administrative procedures, preparing budgets, and designing unit plans and programs. In the more complex forms, the design employed a unit management director and department and a separate administrative hierarchy with authority to supervise the functional department's personnel. While this approach is similar to the use of a "matrix manager," what happened was that the additional hierarchy developed more like a functional department rather than a single matrix manager who was free to range across projects to ensure coordination. The basic unit structure was in line with classic matrix structure where a unit manager becomes a matrix boss and the head nurse becomes a two-boss manager responsible for both the unit manager and the nursing supervisor. As Burns and Wholey describe it, unit managers constitute a horizontal overlay of project managers coordinating all functional personnel on a given clinical area such as surgery, medicine, or pediatrics.

Hospitals were a good choice for this study because, between 1961 and 1978, roughly one-quarter of all large teaching hospitals implemented unit management.[4] One of the great values of this study to a more generalized examination of matrix structures in a wide range of organizations is that the study defines and examines several factors that contribute to the organization's decision to adopt matrix structures and later abandon them. Researchers administered a survey to a panel of hospitals, which included all nonfederal journal hospitals that had either large size (300+ beds) or teaching programs at any point in the panel period. A total of 1,375 hospitals met these criteria and operated continuously over the entire period studied, from 1961 to 1978.

A survey was administered to all of the hospitals on the panel that asked hospital administrators whether or not they had adopted unit management. If the administrators answered the question affirmatively, they were also asked whether or not they had discontinued the program, and in what years they had adopted and abandoned it. The study received an excellent response, with over 90 percent of the sample of the hospitals responding. Of those surveyed, 346 hospitals or 28 percent of those responding had adopted matrix management between 1961 and 1978. Of these, 96 hospitals abandoned matrix management during the same period.[5] Since there were 1,247 questionnaires sent out to the panel, that left 901 hospitals that did not adopt a matrix structure.

Following is a summary of the key results from the study, many of which will play a large role in our later considerations of selecting and managing a more effective matrix.

FACTORS FOR MATRIX ADOPTION

- Organizational diversity
  The complexity of the organization exerted a significant positive effect on adoption. The size of the organization and available resources seemed to have no effect on the decision to adopt matrix management.
- Interorganizational networks
  Gaining knowledge that a prestigious organization had adopted the matrix form exerted significant influence on other organizations to adopt the form as well. Published reports and other general media coverage of the matrix plan also had a great influence on other organizations in the network.
- Regional and local cumulative forces
  The greater the proportion of regional and local organizations adopting matrix management at a given point, the greater the probability that other organizations would adopt it as well.

What emerges from these results seems to fall into two broad categories. The first is that, as organizations become more complex, the need for approaches to information management and decision-making tends to drive the organization toward matrix structures. The second category, which appears equally critical, is that organizations tend to develop matrix structures based on a "follow the leader" principle. This often happens without fully examining the actual need for matrix structures or the ultimate effect, positive or negative, that these changes will have on the organization. In the second category the examples abound. The total quality management initiatives and all of their variants are a case in point. In some cases, "prestigious" organizations move from influence to power by attempting to institutionalize certain approaches across the business community. In the mid to late 1990s, many companies were scrambling to get their ISO 9000 certificates in order to do business with some of their major customers. GE and its commitment to Six Sigma have forced many companies to attempt to adopt the process. Inside GE, Six Sigma is doctrine, and anybody, who wants to either work there or interact effectively with the organization as an outsider, needs to accept and demonstrate their belief in that process.

FACTORS FOR ABANDONING A MATRIX STRUCTURE

This study also looked into factors that influenced the abandonment of matrix structures. What the researchers found was that the same factors that influenced the adoption of a matrix did not necessarily influence the abandonment of a matrix. For example, there was a greater tendency for hospitals with less diversity in their inpatient–outpatient mix to be more likely to abandon the program. Also, the program appeared to be abandoned more frequently by smaller hospitals. Regional cues also played a major role. If several hospitals in a particular region moved away from a matrix structure, other hospitals in that region tended to follow suit. Following are the major factors for matrix abandonment.

- Size of the organizations
    The study suggests that smaller organizations either experienced implementation failure or adopted the program for inappropriate reasons. As such, they later discovered that the matrix program created more problems than it solved or was not necessary to begin with.
- Local network influence
    In the case of abandonment, the organizations were more likely to follow the lead of other organizations abandoning the matrix in the same network, rather than following the lead of more prestigious hospitals in the network.
- Experience with the program
    The abandonment of the matrix program appears to be based more on information derived from direct experience with the matrix program, such as issues of financing, turnover, staffing, and conflict between the various factions in the organization.

This study concludes with a suggestion that the findings have two important implications for team-based approaches to managing quality, which at the time of this study were being implemented in many U.S. industries. The first implication is that the matrix adoption models suggest that organizations implement matrix management primarily for nontechnical reasons, including desires to gain prestige, to emulate larger rivals that have already adopted these forms, and to foster the appearance of quality. Secondly, the matrix abandonment discussion suggests that quality improvement and other efforts may encounter political opposition from vested interests, particularly lower level managers who are likely to resent the loss of power and seek the return to traditional hierarchical arrangements.[6]

As we move forward and look at some of the cases representing successes and failures with matrix management, we can begin to see how many of these same factors come into play regardless of the industry being discussed.

MATRIX MANAGEMENT CASES

As we look into some of the examples of matrix management applications, we begin with one that is working well and has continued to work well for a long period of time. By doing this, we can establish some benchmarks and best practices that may be applicable to other organizations as well. While there are many successful examples out there, the Harley-Davidson Corporation presents a vivid picture of both the application of matrix structure and the type of cultural support necessary to nurture and preserve it.

In the 1970s, plagued by quality problems and an image closely associated with negative stereotypes, Harley-Davidson's production level had reached a new low. For a short period, the company even faced extinction. However, by the 1980s, the leadership at Harley-Davidson realized that survival depended on expanding the business. In order to accomplish this, they determined that they needed to provide excellent products and services to existing customers as well as to significantly increase the customer base.

Beginning with this vision of quality and expanding influence, the company crafted a mission statement that incorporated three main parts:

1. Create an operating environment that supports the belief that employees are the company's only long-term competitive advantage.
2. Empower all employees to achieve full potential through continuous learning and effective career development.
3. Recognize that improvement is continuous and evolving.

More than just lip service, the leadership of the company embarked on a major cultural shift as the centerpiece of its strategy for success. The first strategic initiative called for creation of a culture that encourages empowerment and lifelong learning. In order to accomplish this, Harley-Davidson flattened its hierarchical organizational structure and replaced it with what they termed "business circles." Three business circles were developed: (1) create demand, (2) produce products, and (3) provide support. As part of the cultural change, the company eliminated almost all titles at the senior vice president level and above and employed a consensus-based decision-making model. A high level of interaction between the three business circles was mandated for all decision-making.

The circle structure itself encourages consultation and a highly interdependent culture of cross-functional boundaries. Another by-product of this structure provided (and will continue to provide) exposure for employees to a wide variety of disciplines and gave employees opportunities to demonstrate their talents and contributions. Further, supporting a culture of empowerment was a clear set of values communicated openly and frequently at all levels. Workers were encouraged to take educated risks and challenge ideas coming from all levels during the decision-making process. The constant striving for an egalitarian culture provided access to all levels of management, and individual workers were encouraged to utilize that access.

The second part of the strategy called for the implementation of an effective human resources and performance review strategy that provided developmental opportunities and visibility for all employees. Calling it the PEP (Performance Effectiveness Process), Harley-Davidson expects their employees and managers to have an annual meeting to develop and monitor career development goals. Each quarter, these goals are reviewed, and progress is measured against the mutually agreed upon commitments. One of the goals of the PEP is to provide opportunities for employees to gain cross-functional job experience.

The third strategy involves providing the tools and training necessary to prepare employees to make high-level business decisions. A career development program outlines opportunities for employees to rotate job functions. Formalized programs engage individual workers in cross-functional strategic planning at the highest levels. Where practical and in line with business goals, employees are regularly placed in new teams to learn business skills and engage in cross-functional experiences. Lifelong learning is a core value, and the company supports learning programs that allow all employees to explore new areas of interest and develop their abilities. This is accomplished through a variety of training and educational programs on site and a 100 percent tuition reimbursement plan.

How does this structure and strategy play out with management and staff who live with it day to day in the organization? Meredith Levinson (2000), writing for *CIO Magazine*, provides a picture of how one area of the organization responds and thrives in this heavily matrixed environment. The organizational model of Harley-Davidson's IS department mirrors the overall structure of the company, which, as mentioned earlier, is constructed around three overlapping circles—manufacturing, sales, and support. As such, there are three CIOs, each overseeing the operations for one of the circles. For example, the CIO from manufacturing is responsible for developing the applications and implementing the technologies for all of Harley-Davidson's manufacturing and engineering sites. A second CIO covers the same functions for sales, marketing, and customer service functions, while a third CIO directs the IS for support, including the infrastructure for Harley-Davidson's finance, communication, and legal department. "Although each CIO is in charge of IT for his or her own circle, they share administrative responsibilities, such as recruiting staff, fixing the budget and setting departmental goals."[7]

The risk with this arrangement is that there will be a duplication of effort. Even though each CIO administers issues that are specific to the area of responsibility, there are several IT functions that are germane for all areas. Perhaps because they anticipated this concern, Harley-Davidson added a fourth person with the title of Vice President of Information Systems. These four individuals constitute what the company calls the ISLC (Information Systems Leadership Council). At the beginning of each fiscal year, the three

CIOs set the strategic goals for the IS department making sure that they square with the business goals of the total organization. Given the fact that there is a VP of IS and the fact that the three CIOs report to him or her, it would be easy to call this person the CIO. But he has neither the title nor the function. He is a strategic planner whose role is to evaluate whether IS goals are aligned with the company's business plan.[8] In this arrangement, the VP of IS functions as a true matrix manager. He does not have a staff or a hierarchy, and his primary function is to encourage and monitor collaboration and coordination with the total company's goals and objectives.

This shared responsibility for the organizational model is reflected down through the ranks in the IS function. Additional councils, including the ITC (Information Technology Council) and the ISMC (Information Systems Managers Council), carry the matrix forward. The ISMC is made up of twelve IS managers, who report to the three CIOs.

The ISMC manages and executes projects. They differ from other companies' steering committees and executive oversight committees because they are run by managers. The people who have to execute and sustain a decision are not left out of the decision-making process. They are in fact the decision-makers. This one factor alone may be a major key for opening the door to a successful matrix strategy. One tenet seems to hold true for the full range of organizational productivity: people tend to support actions that are based on decisions that were made with their active participation.

The ITCs ensure that IS is aligned with the mission of the company. Each circle has its own ITC composed of non-IS managers, who report to the VPs in a particular circle. They make decisions on which IS initiatives their circle will take by reviewing business cases and work plans for projects. The ITCs are also responsible for prioritizing IT projects, allocating how each circle will spend its IT budget for the year, and determining the number of people required to execute a project. Levinson points out that the three CIOs acknowledge that managing their IT operations sometimes requires that they park their egos along with their bikes. Managers who are not used to collaboration as a strategy often find this type of approach very difficult. She quotes one of the managers as saying that, "our managers expected this to be a survival of the fittest thing when the strongest person would emerge as the CIO."[9] When problems with a matrix structure arise, one factor is a manager or group of managers who give lip service to supporting the initiative and undermine it at the same time. Acknowledging that that might have been the case at another company, it's not the way it worked at Harley-Davidson. Posted on the walls of every conference room at Harley-Davidson are the company values, including "tell the truth," "keep your promises," and "respect the individual." But the acceptance of these values has to go deeper than wall posters. In many organizations, such postings provide opportunities for cynical laughter.

Apparently, those who have succeeded at Harley-Davidson buy into those values and use them as a guide for the way they work together. At least among members of the IS group there appears to be a strong belief that for this leadership model to succeed, the individuals involved have to be willing to subsume their own ambitions somewhat. The trade-off is the value derived from teamwork. Most IS professionals begin by working in a collaborative environment, but once they get to the senior executive level, they are all alone. A partnership model just makes more sense. I have frequently worked with very talented technical people who have been promoted to management positions and find the shift problematic. Managers who rise in the organization through the technical space do not have the same access to the nuances of management that workers in other communities enjoy.

With some modifications, these principles and approaches of Harley-Davidson continue to the present time. Harley-Davidson clearly represents matrix management's success, and several of the best practices that will be outlined in this book will use the Harley-Davidson model as a springboard. It is also refreshing to tell the Harley-Davidson story since so much of the news surrounding the success or failure of matrix management tends to fall on the failure side.

In an article penned as recently as the November 14, 2005, issue of *Fortune* magazine, the authors discuss the failure of matrix management at AOL by discussing some of the reorganization moves made by Jonathan Miller to realign AOL with the post-Internet boom realities. They talk about his strategy of dividing AOL into four groups. "The move streamlined AOL and eliminated a dreaded matrix management system that had snarled decision making with overlapping responsibilities that enabled countless executives to veto new initiatives."[10] This statement in and of itself belies a misunderstanding of what the matrix is supposed to accomplish. Clearly, if responsibilities overlap, this is an indication of a lack of collaboration. If individual executives have veto power, it is almost impossible for a matrix to succeed. What is being discussed here is a functional organization that was trying to describe itself as a matrix, and when it failed, the matrix became the scapegoat.

Other companies facing the same environmental issues that Harley-Davidson faced in the 1980s did not fare as well with their matrix management initiatives.

THE BAUSCH & LOMB CASE

In many ways, the Bausch & Lomb situation is similar at the outset with what Harley-Davidson was facing. In 1981, Bausch & Lomb's contact lens products division had 55 percent of a $300 million a year U.S. market. The company had experienced nine years of 31 percent compounded average gains before becoming locked in a ferocious price war, which halted profit growth. Rather than making continuous profit, the second-quarter earnings in 1983 dropped 12 percent and the company began to lose money. Daniel Gill, the chief executive at the time, reached out to James Edwards, the head of the instrument group for Bausch & Lomb.

Edwards had demonstrated success at IBM and Xerox and was brought on board to shore up the instrument business for Bausch & Lomb. The instrument business at the time represented 29 percent of company sales, which were $600 million in 1981, but only 13 percent of operating profits. The group was described as a ragtag assembly of some thirty product lines competing against such high-tech heavyweights as PerkinElmer and Hewlett Packard. Edwards came on board with an aggressive plan. In a *Fortune* magazine article titled "Bausch and Lomb's Lost Opportunity," Stratford Sherman outlines the strategy that Edwards attempted to put in place. The first phase of this strategy was a radical overnight reorganization somewhat like Harley-Davidson. Edwards divided manufacturing responsibility among three new divisions: microscopy and image analysis, spectroscopy, and graphics and controls. He created a fourth division to manage all sales and services.

This example shows another application of the "copycat" mentality that drove hospitals in our earlier discussion to jump on unit management because others were doing it. Managers who came into their maturity during the 1980s seem to share this tendency. Rather than seeking out problems and developing effective solutions, they arrive on the scene with a bag full of solutions and then look for problems that fit those predetermined approaches.

Having realigned the levels of authority, Edwards imposed the matrix management style he had learned at IBM. The chief of a manufacturing division retained responsibility for his units' profits or losses but lost control of his sales force. That authority was assigned to the marketing division. Product managers who, until the change, had complete responsibility for a range of goods now became coordinators between the second manufacturing and marketing divisions.

On paper, Edwards reorganization was appealing, because he promised to bring Bausch & Lomb's formerly autonomous businesses into a comprehensible and manageable unit for the first time. Had it worked, this approach would have eliminated such costly redundancies as overlapping research programs, and make better use of the company's position as one of the world's largest analytical-instruments producers.[11]

Unfortunately, Bausch & Lomb's managers did not respond to the plan with the same discipline of IBM managers. Any understanding of the culture at IBM and Xerox of that time would show the flaw in the plan. IBM employees not only dressed the same, they rarely conducted their social lives outside of the IBM community. One can argue whether this loss of individuality and adventure is good for the long term, but these people knew how to collaborate. The Xerox headquarters that I visited during this time offered a complete lifestyle twenty four hours a day, seven days a week. There was food, recreation, health club facilities, and generally comfortable accommodations. If so inclined, an employee could find that most of his or her needs were met without ever having to leave the building.

Another problem with the plan, as one former executive points out, Edwards didn't do his homework on Bausch & Lomb with regards to the expertise necessary to sell certain products. Salesmen of simple microscopes were now put into the position of having to sell complex, computer-driven chemical analysis devices. Even though a major campaign for the matrix structure was mounted and brochures and videotapes explaining the changes were circulated throughout the group, many employees and key managers remained confused and demoralized.

Instead of saving money and raising earnings as Daniel Gill had hoped, the instruments group continued to lose money. The budget of the expanded sales division was out of control, and the recession at the time was causing problems with the group's primary customers. Operating income went from $1.3 million in the first quarter to a $3 million loss.

Edwards left Bausch & Lomb coincident with an announced loss of 32 percent in net income for the third quarter of 1982. The CEO, Gill, told analysts in New York that all four instrument division presidents would now report directly to him to ensure that the turnaround of the business was achieved in short order. Focusing on short-term cost reduction, he fired hundreds of sales and production employees. He returned sales responsibility to the graphics division and made a hash of the matrix management concept.

Sherman offers this opinion about the danger of employing a matrix management system:

Introducing a complex new system of management is always risky and the appeal of matrix management has lately dimmed for even some of its best known adherents, notably Texas Instruments. The turn around at BL was certainly not aided by Edwards's incautious execution of his programs—or by Gill's lack of staying power. When they said, "make haste slowly," the Romans might have been talking about corporate management.[12]

So, matrix management is once again seen as the culprit rather than a misperception of management that organizations have cultures that can be rapidly manipulated and changed with bold, sweeping actions. Organizations "are" cultures, and, as such, need to evolve change organically rather than having it thrust upon them.

HIGH-LEVEL MATRIX MANAGEMENT BEST PRACTICES

We begin our discussion of matrix management best practices by reviewing in more detail the recent study conducted by Sy and D'Annunzio mentioned earlier. The results of the study were published in 2005 and were based on surveys, interviews, and workshops conducted with 194 top-level and mid-level managers from seven major multinational corporations in six industries. As management consultants, Sy and D'Annunzio had access to several clients of their firm. They were also able to bring an in-depth perception of the organization since they were very familiar with all aspects of the business. The industries represented were automotive, chemical, computer hardware and services, financial, oil and gas, and technology products and solutions. The companies studied had a varying range of experience with matrix management. Some had operated within a matrix structure for three years, while others had been using the form for more than twenty years.[13]

The results of this study are important for several reasons. First, it is a contemporary study that looks at organizations currently experiencing the dynamics of matrix management. In addition, the fairly wide sampling of industries adds relevance to any generalized conclusions. Secondly, the study used participants at different management levels and employed multiple methodologies to strengthen the validity of the findings. Thirdly, I have had the opportunity to work with one of the principal investigators of the study (D'Annunzio) and have a high degree of respect for the quality and thoroughness of her research.

The study found that although each company experienced unique obstacles, there were many similarities that occurred when adopting a matrix strategy. The researchers identified five common challenges.

1. Misaligned goals
2. Unclear roles and responsibilities
3. Ambiguous authority
4. Lack of a matrix guardian
5. Silo-focused employees

These categories capture the greater part of the universe of matrix problems.

Misaligned Goals

One curious finding was that more top-level managers cited misalignment of goals as a challenge than mid-level managers. The researchers concluded that this finding was a matter of focus and that most business goals and objectives are developed at top management levels. What is somewhat unclear in the results is that the top managers did not indicate if the misalignment of goals was between themselves and lower levels of the organization or between the top managers. Despite the differences and perceptions on this issue, the participants in the study at all levels seem to agree that the following factors provided difficulty in goal alignment.

- Competing or conflicting objectives between matrix dimensions.
- Inadequate processes to align goals and detect possible misalignments.
- Lack of synchronization, coordination, and poor timing of work plans and objectives.
- Insufficient communication and consultation between matrix dimensions.[14]

Among those participants who felt they had successfully dealt with the problem of conflicting goals, two remedies stood out. The first was the use of instrumentation such as spreadsheets that accumulated all of the goals derived from each year's planning and cascaded them vertically and horizontally throughout the organization. When this was properly done, the goals of one unit always reinforced or at least were in line with the goals of other units. The value of instrumentation as part of a matrix is unquestionable. One caution, however, is that instrumentation is not a substitute for interpersonal interaction.

The second factor is more elusive, but no less important. Many senior leaders say that the secret to success is to communicate constantly the company's vision and objectives to the employees. "As employees strive to achieve contradictory objectives, a certain amount of discord is bound to filter through the rank and file. Constant communication of company vision and objectives helps to minimize this discord and clarifies any lingering ambiguity because the communication serves as a beacon in aligning goals and objectives."[15] Of course, the assumption here is that the vision is shared throughout the culture in large measure, that it is tied to something the culture already accepts, and the communication, both formal and informal, is engaging without being overly directive.

Unclear Roles and Responsibilities

A major stumbling block of the matrix is not knowing what your role is. This also ties to communication. Each manager is responsible for clarifying roles and responsibilities for everyone on the team. The study shows that 87 percent of mid-level managers polled cite unclear goals and responsibilities as a major issue. This is out of sync with top-level managers, with only 23 percent of them reporting the same difficulty. Ambiguous roles and responsibilities are a major problem for mid-level managers. They cited the following primary issues.

- Unclear job descriptions and guidelines on roles and responsibilities.
- Ambiguous roles and responsibilities, which create tension among employees.
- Confusion over who is the boss.
- Not knowing who to contact for information.

This research, as well as much of the research done by me, points to this ambiguity of roles and responsibilities as being a major problem. When the business environment demands change, top managers expect middle managers and employees to adapt quickly to the new demands. A common complaint from top managers is that middle managers and employees are not taking the initiative to define solutions to the problems as they occur. At the same time, the employees are looking for direction and clarity from

the top managers. Those companies that manage the matrix most ε
provide clear guidelines and descriptions on roles and responsibilit
accountability for business objectives, provide a single point of conιαcι ιʋι
information or approval for areas of responsibility, and create mechanisms
for information sharing.

Again, some type of instrumentation comes into play. Some organizations
continue to use the RASIC tool developed during the early days of matrix
management in the aerospace industry. RASIC is an acronym standing for
Responsible, Approve, Support, Inform, and Consult. This tool is described
in more detail in Appendix A; however, when used effectively, it goes a long
way toward keeping roles and responsibilities defined.

Ambiguous Authority

This finding appears to be closely aligned with the issues of roles and
responsibilities previously discussed. This study refers to it separately
because in the matrix, designated leaders often are assigned responsibility
without authority as a result of the dual reporting structure. On this issue,
both top-level and mid-level managers agree that ambiguous authority is a
common dilemma. The findings show the following difficulties:

- Confusion over who has the final authority.
- Lack of clarity on areas of accountability.
- Leaders unaccustomed to sharing decision-making.
- Delay in the decision-making process.

While all of these hit the mark, the delay in the decision-making process is
clearly damaging, because one of the key benefits of a well-functioning matrix
is speedier decision-making.

Resolving issues of authority depend greatly on the existing corporate culture. Where the culture supports a collaborative approach to problem solving,
informal networks and more formalized negotiation are effective in resolving
this issue. In organizations where the culture is more individualized and
political, there is a tendency for functional units to hold rank and work hard
for the maintenance of their status and power rather than resolve the issues.
Mid-level managers in this study reported that senior leaders often fail to provide the level of authority they need, because they either reverse decisions
after the fact or do not allow local leaders to make decision in the first place.[16]
Decision reversal is deadly to a matrix. Once burned on a decision, mid-level
managers develop an understandable reluctance to make any decisions at all.

Lack of a Matrix Guardian

Another interesting finding from this study was that few companies actually
tracked the performance of their matrix structure to understand how well it

was operating. Again, research by me concurs in this finding. In fact, there are many examples where metrics (surveys, interviews, and the like) have been conducted to assess the organizational climate only to have the results suppressed because they did not reflect a positive outlook. The lack of a matrix guardian was cited by 92 percent of top-level managers in this study as a major hindrance to performance. These were the key findings:

- Lack of consequences and rewards for matrix performance fails to motivate employees to make the matrix work.
- Failure to establish and maintain a monitoring process to detect and identify matrix performance problems (because employees are reluctant to divulge problems associated with their unit).
- Not ensuring the matrix guardian has senior level support and authority to take action.
- Not preserving the objectivity of the matrix guardian and preventing undue political pressure.

High-performing organizations that were studied employ a matrix guardian. This person is charged with identifying best practices and ensuring that they are disseminated throughout the company. He or she is also well respected within the organization. Having this individual report directly to the CEO alleviates political influences and other obstacles that keep important issues from surfacing. Highly matrixed organizations need this matrix guardian or matrix manager to ensure that collaboration is facilitated between the project teams and the functional departments. This person also needs to be "fireproof" to ensure that his or her actions are not hindered by stepping on political toes.

Silo-Focused Employees

It will come as no surprise that most employees at all levels demonstrated a loyalty and cohesion to their subunit within the organization. Their behavior tends to support the objectives and concerns with the subunit, even when it could be detrimental to the organization as a whole. Participants in this study at all levels agreed on these issues:

- Personal conflicts between leaders that hinder collaboration between units.
- Withholding resources from others.
- Lack of trust between employees in different business units.
- Employees lack the requisite skills to function in the matrix.
- Insufficient communication between different business units.

This study concluded with a discussion of several best practices adopted by successful matrix organizations. These best practices are listed here and will be added to, developed, and expanded as this book progresses.

- Define expectations
- Provide training
- Work across functions
- Build relationships

These best practices and others that we will discuss later on provide the backdrop for the development and maintenance of a successful matrix management initiative. However, the same theme continues to develop. The four high-level best practices that came out of this study are, arguably, all relationship-based actions. One of the highlights of the study is putting training in the forefront as one of the key components of success. This echoes the opinion of the earliest matrix theorists but has been conspicuously absent from more recent analyses of matrix forms. Confusion, lack of clarity, ambiguity, insufficient communication, and the lack of requisite skills continually emerge as the major roadblocks to successful implementation of the matrix form. Good training is part of the solution. People cannot comfortably change their behavior because they don't have the necessary tools and techniques to develop a comfort level with the new demands.

In the next section, we shift our focus from theory and understanding to analysis and implantation.

PART II

Embracing the Matrix

It is difficult to draw a hard line between theory and practice when talking about organizational structure and design. In previous chapters, we looked at examples of implementations of matrix management to help illustrate theoretical aspects of the process and gain an understanding of the inherent complexity and the factors that influence the success and failure of matrix management. In this part, the intent is to shift the emphasis toward strategies for implementing matrix management, improving the matrix structures that already exist, or making an informed decision not to move your organization in that direction.

Ronald Ashkenas (1994) tells the story of a global manufacturing company that was experiencing declining market share due to downturns in the residential housing and building markets. Unable to cut costs fast enough or develop new products or markets, the company gradually slipped into the red. To counter this trend, senior management launched several initiatives in the course of eighteen months.

- A customer satisfaction survey;
- An employee satisfaction survey;
- A Baldrige Award–type process, complete with large-scale audits and an internal panel of judges;
- Across-the-board quality training and dozens of quality action teams;
- Kaizen training and manufacturing floor redesign;
- Activity-based accounting;
- A strategic measurement process with a team of "experts" that moved through each department developing measurement "levels";

- A senior "visioning" team to compare the future state with the current situation and do "interactive planning" to close the gap;
- A "bureaucracy-busting" team to root out unnecessary forms, meetings, and administration;
- A major information systems project to integrate the order entry and production scheduling systems;
- Socio-technical training in several plants;
- A project to achieve ISO 9000 certification; and
- Personal productivity training for managers based on a recent management "best seller."

While many of the programs provided powerful tools, they only produced isolated gains, which did not add up to a turnaround of the division. In fact, with so many people engaged in these activities and feeling overworked by their involvement, a number of senior managers began to believe that the fundamental problem was lack of resources. In reality, the division's costs had gotten completely out of hand, and the corporate parent was forced to intervene with the demand for a painful across-the-board expense reduction. Eventually, a new senior manager canceled most of the ongoing change programs and refocused the organization on cost reduction and product development. Six months later, the division was back in the black. The simple focus on a few key results—given in clear, "no-choice" terms—accomplished what more than a dozen "improvement" programs could not.[1]

Throwing solutions at a problem is not unique to this company. The track record of successes with change initiatives is not stellar. Having said that, and despite its checkered history, matrix management is not a fad. It is a reality thrust upon many organizations that want to compete in the fast changing, complex business environment of today. Change is continuous and never-ending. To keep up, managers at all levels need to see themselves as change agents. To be a successful change agent, a manager requires a shift of focus from programs to results.

Chapter 5 asks the reader to begin by searching out matrix elements that already exist within the organization and asks questions about how these collaborative entities are performing. Chapter 6 offers a view of leadership that is necessary in order to nurture and support the flexibility and innovation needed to succeed today. Chapter 7 looks at the special issues and concerns of the project manager—the key player in any matrix management scheme. Chapter 8 continues to focus on the project manager from the point of view of management style and how the human element factors into project outcomes. Chapter 9 looks at the unique challenges created by matrix management across borders, multiculturalism, and strategic alliances. Finally, Chapter 10 expands and summarizes best practices and presents a blueprint for success with matrix forms.

CHAPTER 5

Discovering Your Organization's Matrix

> Dear Professor Hunt, Our new chief executive has been turning the company upside down and the process has been traumatic. The old reporting structures have gone—instead we now have much looser "matrices." If you try to pin down the management consultants who are advising him about how it's supposed to work, they answer with terms like "dual axis" and "self regulation." The whole thing looks to me—as one of the managers who has to implement the new structure—like a recipe for chaos. Are matrix structures likely to be a passing fad? I've read that some companies are already abandoning them.
>
> —John W. Hunt[1]

It is a major premise of this book that if you are involved in an organization of any size, a matrix form probably already exists within your structure. As with most things, anyone seriously considering an examination of the potential business benefits from employing a matrix must first discover how matrices are or are not currently functioning within the organization. Matrix forms are a natural hybrid; they are difficult to pigeonhole. They will vary according to the type of organization, the needs of the business, the acceptance level of the employees, the enthusiasm or lack thereof from top management, and a myriad of other factors that influence the ultimate shape.

Common examples of matrix management almost exclusively focus attention on the relationship between the functional manager and the project manager. As we move forward in this chapter, we will broaden our view about how matrices operate within the organization. However, we shouldn't undermine the primary importance of this bipolar managerial arrangement.

Whenever the two-boss situation is encountered, there are always questions about who is the real boss? On paper, the equal division of responsibility appears as a fait accompli. In reality, something very different occurs. Many theorists as well as practitioners disagree as to whether a balance of power is necessary or even desirable. Even in a situation where a balance of power is mandated, employees may still perceive the functional manager as the "real" boss because he or she shares the employee's discipline, is located closer geographically, and may even have been responsible for the hiring decision that brought the employee on board. Also, the functional manager often retains responsibility for performance appraisals, raises, and promotions. In other cases, some employees may identify so strongly with a particular project that they see the project manager as their boss. At the heart of the operation of the matrix is the balance of power.

Theoretically, it should be possible to divide the authority and responsibility more or less equally between the project and the functional managers; in practice, however, this is difficult and seldom occurs. It is one thing to lay out where the major responsibilities of both parties are, but very difficult to ensure that this results in a balance of power. As one researcher puts it,

In fact there are many reasons why it is almost impossible to have a truly equal balance of power between functional and project management. Not the least of these reasons is the fact that we are dealing with people, and that all people, including managers, are different.[2]

If you are a conscientious, knowledgeable project manager, your concerns are going to drift toward becoming involved in how and when the task will be done. You wouldn't want to wait for functional management to make every technical decision. In his book on project management, Linn Stuckenbruck (1981) discusses the project manager's point of view.

The project manager must ensure that technical decisions are made on schedule, and then must review the key technical decisions and challenge them if necessary. As project integrator, he or she has the overriding responsibility for evaluating every key project decision to determine how it interfaces with the other project tasks, and with the schedule and budget. The project manager therefore must get involved and influence every project action, and, as a last resort, always has appeal rights or veto power—for the good of the project. The project manager even gets involved in "who will do the task?" After all, the highest achievers and most innovative personnel in the discipline organizations will be highly sought after, and the project managers will seek to obtain only the very best people for their projects.[3]

Stuckenbruck then goes on to illuminate the points of contention that naturally arise between project and functional managers.

Functional managers will inevitably get involved in other details like, "what, when, and for how much?" They also have a strong personal interest in these details because they are tied to the organization's performance including project schedules and budgets. They see themselves as the overseers for monitoring whether a project is technically feasible or realistically prices. Since the project, program, or product is important to the success of the company, one would think the project managers would always have the scale of power tipped in their direction, with firm support of top management—"Not necessarily so. In fact, not usually so, at least in a matrix organization."[4]

In its most advanced form, matrix management does put the balance of power in the hands of the project manager. However, in less advanced forms, functional managers have powerful forces on their side. As previously pointed out, the functional manager is normally perceived by project personnel to be the real boss. After all, the general perception is that functional management is part of the unchanging ladder in the management hierarchy and is therefore perceived to be "permanent" by the employees. The functional organization represents home base, to which project personnel expect to return after the completion of the project.

If the matrix is to succeed, it requires more than a balance of power. Even very strong support from upper management will not guarantee that the initiative will be conducted successfully. The key is the relationship between the project and the individual functional managers. Building and conducting these relationships so that they operate in a positive and contributory way is the major organizational challenge. As we look at the various manifestations of the matrix that currently exist in the organization, we need to keep that point in mind.

Despite the wide variety of permutations that the matrix can take, there are three variants of matrix design that serve as guideposts and have received some common acceptance among several of the primary matrix management theorists including Galbraith, who was the first to describe them. This three-part definition, which includes "functional matrix," "balanced matrix," and "project matrix," was more recently used by Sy and D'Annunzio in their study as discussed in Chapter 4. The explanations of each category that follow are my compilation of the available range of thinking on these descriptions.

FUNCTIONAL MATRIX

The functional matrix is also referred to as a "weak matrix." In this form, the organization retains most of the characteristics of a pure functional organization. It follows the classical hierarchical management model. The functions of the organization are separated, and each employee reports to a supervisor in that function. A functional matrix occurs when an individual is designated as either a project manager or a project administrator and is assigned to oversee cross-functional aspects of a project. To support this effort, there is encouragement in the environment for cross-functional collaboration, which often takes the form of processes and procedures designed to help facilitate the interchange of communication.

Within a functional matrix, the functional managers maintain control over their resources and project areas. The project manager has only limited authority over members of the team and primarily plays a coordinating role. A functional or weak matrix has been described by project managers as one in which the balance of power tilts decisively in the direction of line or functional management.

The functional matrix has certain advantages and could very well be the right choice depending on what the objectives of the organization might be. Because the decision-making authority lies within the functional units, it is possible to enforce standards across various projects because the function has complete control over each segment of the project. In addition, by concentrating experts within departments, there is less redundancy of resources. However, the functional matrix retains most of the problems that are often associated with a pure functional organization. These include an inherent slowness to react to environmental changes and a lack of flexibility of communication when attempting to collaborate across functions.

In the course of working with cross-functional teams at a major national laboratory, I experienced first hand some of the issues surrounding the functional matrix. The dilemma for this laboratory is the conflict between a very rigid segmented divisional structure and a need to employ a broader range of cross-functional resources in order to respond rapidly to the changing needs of its customer base. Each of the divisions has different funding sources. The functional managers are rated based upon the amount of funding they are able to bring into their divisions.

Because of budgetary and other constraints, there is little incentive for managers to assign staff members as participants on cross-functional projects where there is no clear financial return to the division. Because there is a mandate to participate at some level in these cross-functional teams, functional managers respond in different ways. There are those managers who believe in collaboration and support the fact that potential future technologies discovered by these cross-functional teams will have a positive impact in the long run, both on the laboratory as a whole and on their specific departments. Those managers allow for a concentrated short-term staff commitment to these projects.

At the other end of the spectrum are those managers who have little or no interest in the cross-functional project or its objectives and see the project merely as a resource drain on personnel and expertise that could be better used elsewhere. Their response is to either opt out entirely or assign staff members on an availability basis. A resource may be assigned to the project team for a period of time and then either swapped or completely removed from the team because a "more important job" has become available in the division.

A third and perhaps most prevalent form of management response comes from those functional managers who neither support nor oppose the objectives of the project team. However, they are confused about purpose and direction the team is taking as well as about the deliverables that might be expected. These mangers may assign staff to the team for the duration of the project; however, they periodically insert themselves into the team process and often succeed in confusing the team members and impeding progress.

The project manager in a functional matrix is often in an unenviable position since he or she has little control over the staffing of the team and little authority to provide either reward or sanction to its members. The task of coordinating the team's efforts often becomes overwhelming. Pressured by time and the need to produce tangible results, project mangers in these situations often end up doing most of the work on their own without the benefit that a coordinated team effort could provide.

Functional matrix approaches work best at higher levels in the organization. If a team is made up of functional managers, there is little need for a project manager with authority. All of the decision-making power is already in the room. The project manager, who could be one of the functional managers, acts as a facilitator and structures, monitors, and encourages the communication while keeping people on track. In our earlier discussion of the Harley-Davidson model, we saw an example of how the functional matrix works at the management level. Many organizations today have some form of functional matrix working with varying degrees of success. Looking for the functional matrices in the organization is a good way to begin an analysis of how the matrix is operating generally within the overall structure.

BALANCED MATRIX

The balanced matrix is sometimes referred to as the classic matrix model. This is actually a misnomer. When the origins of matrix management are traced back to the aerospace industry, it is clear that the earliest forms were not "balanced." A good case in point is the McDonnell Aircraft Corporation in the 1950s. While the term "matrix organization" did not appear in the vernacular until the 1960s, its origins can be traced to the development of "program management."

McDonnell in the 1950s was moved toward being a product organization by a combination of external factors. The Armed Services Procurement Act allowed the defense department to award sole-source contracts and gave McDonnell more control over its subcontractors. It was also a time when McDonnell was receiving more missile contracts, which was a new technology both for McDonnell and for the armed services. As a result, the oversight functions that were currently in place did not work effectively for missile contracts.

Another factor was the pressure to develop products in a relatively short period of time and the requirement that training begin before an aircraft design was completed. This practice precluded a clean hand off from one department to the next. Perhaps most important, McDonnell's customers adopted a product-oriented structure. In 1952, the Air Force reorganized its design engineers into the ARDC (Air Research and Development Command). The Air Force then formed Weapon System Project Offices to ease the transfer of oversight from the ARDC to the Air Material Command responsible for maintenance. Because McDonnell at that point answered to only one office, the Air Force wanted only one McDonnell employee answering to them. J. S. McDonnell, the president, spent most of his time answering to the shareholders, so he designated a deputy to gather information from the departments in order to brief the Air Force Weapons System Project Officer. In this way, information was centralized and the first stage of program management came into being.

In this truly classic matrix form, the program manager had significant authority. The program manager led the conceptual design of the aircraft and defined the contract with the customer. The program manager then delegated portions of the contract to the departments and pressured them to do the work on time, to specifications, without billing the project contract for more materials and hours than were budgeted. In this position, the program manager was closely allied with the customer and the weapons system rather than the shareholders and their capital.

This arrangement did not reflect what we have come to understand as a balanced matrix. In a balanced matrix, decision-making authority rests equally between project managers and functional managers. While the program manager had significant control over the design and development of the product, he had no mandated authority to mediate technical disputes between the departments. When conflicts arose, only the departments had an overhead budget and sufficient manpower to engage in battle. As a result, the program team would have to wait out the resolution of the conflict and accept the solution suggested by the departments. The problem, then, was the conflict between the departments rather than conflict between the departments and the program manager. Finding this gridlock unacceptable, in 1958, program managers were permitted to hire more engineers. As a result, the program teams began to do more line work and the departments more staff work. Program managers had their own payroll and could select personnel who were better trained in certain technologies.

The same year McDonnell also created the position of General Manager with status comparable to that of department heads. This General Manager represented all of the program managers in discussions with the President. By the late 1950s, McDonnell could be termed as a balanced matrix organization with neither departments nor programs defining the line product of the firm. Within this matrix organization, the departments served as repositories for expertise in areas such as manufacturing methods, purchasing, financial accounting, sales and support, testing and quality control, and various engineering disciplines. Departments billed for their specialized expertise and sold this expertise to any program group needing help on a new type of aircraft. It was, however, the various programs that were the profit centers within the corporation, and the departments served as the cost centers. The programs controlled the contract funds and determined whether work would be assigned to departments, work would be awarded to an outside firm under subcontract, or advice would be requested from defense department engineers.

The balanced matrix can take many forms; however, there are some key characteristics that differentiate it from the functional matrix. Rather than being full members reporting directly and continuously to functional managers, employees are actually members of two organizing dimensions within the company. The functional departments provide a sector for secure, stable career advancement. Each staff member is evaluated by two bosses—his or her functional manager and the project manager to whom he or she has been assigned for periods of time. While a staff member's time is owned by the functional department, it is billed by the project. When a project ends, the staff member goes back into departmental overhead where he or she is expected to update technical expertise and analyze the learning achieved in solving the project problem. A balanced matrix has to be managed effectively since the dynamics of this form open up the possibility of power struggles between the functional side and the project side of an organization.

PROJECT MATRIX

The term project matrix is descriptive of how the balance of power shifts from the functional manager in a functional matrix to shared authority in a balanced matrix and finally to the center of authority being placed on the project manager. As with the balanced matrix, there is a need for horizontal and vertical coordination. However, project managers become alternative authority figures to those with hierarchical position power.

A project matrix is most effective in organizations where tasks are assigned to projects of limited duration but need to develop results quickly. These projects enjoy a high degree of decision-making autonomy. In its most mature form, a project matrix moves from a temporary to a permanent task orientation. The project manager at this stage becomes a product manager, or a mini general manager. He or she is responsible for the complete business, including its profit and loss, its success and failure, and its future potential. Staff members in the project matrix are seen as fully functioning members of both the department and the project. Functional and project managers contribute equally to the employees' evaluation. However, the rewarding of recognition such as offices or titles is the purview of the project manager. Another characteristic of project matrix organizations is the existence of comprehensive team building and interpersonal skill development programs. Information flows freely throughout the organization. Managerial roles are reassessed and result in lower specificity. The physical space reflects the organizational structure. It is not unusual for project managers to maintain operational space in two or more places. This is also true of functional personnel who have been assigned to a project. They are expected to physically move their locations as they phase in and out of projects or programs.

Team participation, rather than being a temporary assignment, becomes an everyday way of life. Rather than being stable entities, functions within the organization also change and develop because of new demands. For example, the marketing of a product internationally might require the development of a function exhibiting language and cultural expertise. Product managers often acquire the right to subcontract outside the organization for services that could be supplied in-house but in some way do not meet the specific requirements. The same is true of functional groups who can also sell their services outside. This regular sojourn into the environment outside of the organization supplies the system with much needed feedback as well as information on trends.

The project matrix does not eliminate competition and conflict between the product side of the organization and the functional areas. It is one of the primary objectives of the CEO to manage the balance of power between these two entities. Kolodny (1979) summarizes this effectively:

If economic times are tight, power shifts to the product side which is more closely concerned with profit and loss and short term performance. If the economy is benevolent, the emphasis shifts to new developments in the sub environments of the functional areas since competitors will also be examining the new technologies, and new developments that will ultimately allow projects and programs to formulate innovative responses to their product-market sectors.[5]

A key change for functional managers is to become proactive rather than reactive. They frequently interact with product and project managers and try to anticipate their needs. The role of the functional manager becomes more focused on support, while they do retain control over much of the team responsible for carrying out plans and controls established by project managers.

WHAT TYPE OF MATRIX DOES YOUR ORGANIZATION HAVE?

Chances are your organization will not fit neatly within any of the three categories mentioned above. In larger organizations, it is possible for various divisions to operate under a different matrix scheme. Depending on the types of products and the needs of the marketplace being served by each division, it is possible that a scattered matrix arrangement of this type can be successful. It is not likely.

Very often the results of this kind of arrangement can be seen following an acquisition. Consider this scenario: A large functionally oriented organization acquires a smaller entrepreneurial firm to help expand its market, increase innovation, and set a new direction for the future. More times than not, these acquisitions or mergers are disappointing. The larger, functional organization imposes policies, procedures, reporting relationships, and lines of communication on what was perhaps a more project-centered collegial organization. The resulting clash of cultures stifles the innovation and creativity of the smaller company, stimulates an exodus of key personnel, and ultimately produces a disappointing outcome.

In recent years, much of this activity has taken place in the financial services sector. In a bid to expand its customer base and service offerings, the MONY Group acquired several smaller entrepreneurial firms ranging from brokerage to accounting and financial planning. These acquisitions continued to operate for some time with a high degree of autonomy. As MONY prepared for the acquisition by AXA, all of these smaller firms lost autonomy and were ultimately absorbed in the larger entity. In July 2004, the MONY Group in turn was acquired by AXA Financial, Inc. AXA almost immediately set about realigning the expanded organization to focus more on its core business of life insurance and annuities.

In September 2005, it was announced that Merrill Lynch intended to buy Advest Group, a subsidiary of the former MONY Group, from AXA. Dow Jones Newswires announced the pending deal on September 14, 2005, and quoted Russ Alan Prince (2005), a consultant to brokerage firms, commenting on results of the merger, "Advest brokers may resist the Merrill model of selling ancillary products such as mortgages and insurance and may balk at trading the collegial atmosphere at a small firm for Merrill's more regimented ways."[6] Prince's comment reflects an understanding of what often happens when there is a serious disconnect between core cultural values. This is another example of the potential downside to ignoring the durability of a culture.

FIND THE MATRIX

Where are the matrices in your organization? It is useful to start with a quick inventory of your own organizational structure. This investigation leads toward an understanding of whether your organization is generally receptive to matrix forms, and, if they do exit, where they might be found. The following inventory asks some basic questions about what it's like to work where you are. If you are a top manager in the organization, it would be very useful for your understanding and perspective if you administered this brief survey to others in your organization in various functions and at different levels. Anyone considering establishing or more effectively managing a matrix must be aware of gaps in the perception of how the organization is currently progressing. My experience has shown that there is often a wide disparity between the way the various levels and segments of the organization view the general organizational climate.

...IZATION QUICK INVENTORY

The scores break out into three groups: structure, culture, and risk tolerance. These three dimensions give a quick snapshot of the way you perceive your organization. For example, a high "structure" score suggests a perception of a more centralized, control-oriented structure. Of course, that doesn't mean that matrices do not exist. However, against the backdrop of command and control, they may be having a difficult time functioning effectively.

If your organization is highly structured, you will most likely find matrix activity in the form of special projects, or other teams and work groups with cross-functional members working outside of the mainstream. There may also be some informal matrix activity such as of internal interest groups and other mechanisms for cross-functional information sharing. Special projects may or may not be long-term initiatives. They generally grow out of a felt need for specific problem solving or innovations and are most often supported by a powerful member of the management team. Since they are highly dependent on continued support for their existence, they are rapidly dismantled when that support is withdrawn.

Informal matrix initiatives can contribute significantly to the overall learning of the organization, but they have little or no authority to effect

Table 5.1
Organization Quick Inventory

___1.	Most decisions come from the top.
___2.	There is a dominant organizational culture.
___3.	Innovation is encouraged.
___4.	A few people make most of the decisions.
___5.	The organization has many subgroups and cliques.
___6.	Most of the attention is focused on efficiency.
___7.	We hold a "cutting-edge" position in our industry.
___8.	Different points of view are encouraged.
___9.	Individual contributors are empowered to make decisions.
___10.	Idea generation is heavily supervised.
___11.	The organization embraces risk-taking.
___12.	Policies and procedures are always at the forefront.
___13.	Working independently is supported by management.

Use the following scale for each statement.
(1) Strongly Disagree, (2) Disagree, (3) Neutral, (4) Agree, and (5) Strongly Agree.

Figure 5.1
Organization Quick Survey Score Sheet

1			**Structure**
4			4–10 Low
9	Reverse score (e.g., 5=1 and 2=4)		11–15 Moderate
12			16–20 High
		Total	
2			**Culture**
5	Reverse score		4–10 Project Matrix
8	Reverse score		11–15 Balanced Matrix
13	Reverse score		16–20 Functional Matrix
		Total	
3			**Risk Tolerance**
6	Reverse score		5–11 Low Risk
7			12–17 Moderate
10			18–25 Innovative
11			
		Total	

Place your scores in the score column for the appropriate question and add them up in the total box.

change. A low score on structure does not automatically mean a more supportive environment for matrix systems. One of the characteristics of a fully functioning matrix is structural flexibility, but a lot of early adopters of matrix management made the mistake of decentralizing the structure and failing to identify individuals who would be responsible for administering and monitoring the matrix. Rather than leading to higher productivity, collaboration, and innovation, many organizations found that decentralization created costly redundancies and turf wars that crippled decision-making.

A high or low score on culture does not indicate whether the organization has a culture or not. All organizations have a culture. Rather, what this score seeks to point out is the level of constraint that the culture places upon innovative approaches to structure. A low score on this particular dimension suggests that the organization could be receptive to the flexibility provided by a project matrix form. Conversely, a high score might indicate that there is a strong adherence to a functional arrangement, and more flexible forms are not encouraged.

The third dimension, which we are calling risk tolerance, provides a quick measure of how the organization deals with strategy. In this case, the higher the score the more the organization might be open to taking risks that lead to innovation. Of course, this little inventory is not a comprehensive diagnostic tool. Its usefulness is in establishing a focus on the organization with an eye toward where matrix forms might be found.

As we discussed earlier, matrix management made a big splash in the 1970s. For the most part, that splash turned out to be a belly flop. Although there are plentiful matrix structures in operation today, they are rarely talked about even within the organization. Companies using matrix structures tend to keep quiet about it. These structures have become the "stealth" design of the past ten years. Although not recognized, matrix management is often delivering results far more effectively in an environment far more attuned to its structural peculiarities than when it was first introduced. This is not a surprise, today's global economic environment, along with major transitions in both the culture of organizations and its workforce, fits better with matrix requirements. Most companies no longer have long product cycles and need to update their offerings frequently or perish. For many companies, the formula for success today is a flat, lean, team organization, focused around business processes that cut across all the functional areas and are driven by customer satisfaction and product improvement.

As we go forward in our analysis of existing matrices within the organization, we will look at five ways in which a matrix may be generated. These are planned matrix, accidental matrix, spontaneous matrix, isolated matrix, and informal matrix. These terms relate to the way in which each of the matrix forms came into being in the organization. For diagnostic purposes, it is assumed that the matrix has not been formally initiated by top management as a mandated change in structure and reporting relationships. In that case, the matrix is obvious, so we don't have to search for it. Managing and, in most cases, healing a mandated matrix is a subject we will address later in the book. Our interest here lies with the discovery of matrix configurations that currently exist within the organization without the fanfare of formal implementations.

Planned Matrix

Figure 5.2 provides an example of one type of planned matrix. In this case, one functional manager is given a problem that requires input from most or all of the other functional areas. As an example, a CFO may be required to overhaul the accounts receivable and accounts payable processes in the company. In order to accomplish this effectively, he or she needs the input and collaboration of the IT, manufacturing, and sales departments in order to provide a comprehensive solution. In one example, the CFO takes on the role of project coordinator and asks the other functional managers to suggest staff members whom they feel will be able to provide the necessary input. In a typical scenario, the CFO might kick off the first meeting, get some ideas about how to proceed from the participants, set up an action plan,

Figure 5.2
Planned Matrix

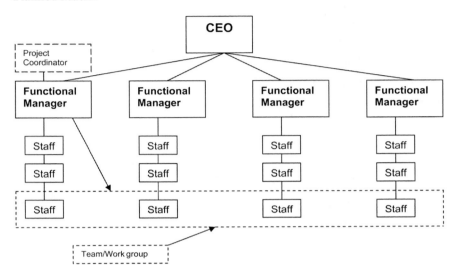

and then allow the participants to move forward on their own. The expectation is that they will come up with a collaborative solution and report back to the CFO with what they believe is a workable plan. In this type of planned matrix, all of the authority and responsibility for the ultimate outcome remains with the functional manager. In one variant, he or she may appoint a staff member with a direct reporting relationship as project coordinator or team leader. I call this a planned matrix since it is created out of a felt need for collaboration to address an issue that impacts all of the various functions. It is surprising how many of these planned matrices already exist in most organizations. Here are some of the places to look.

- Implementation of new technology will require collaboration from all the functional units that may be affected by this change.
- Changes in processes and procedures such as hiring a travel management company to help consolidate and control costs.
- A company-wide training program such as a diversity initiative or change in performance appraisal, policies, and procedures.
- Relocation or other physical space issues require significant collaboration between all of the areas affected by the move.

All of these scenarios and many others share one primary characteristic: they are initiated by one functional area and are charged with the responsibility of finding solutions to a very specific problem. Whether called teams, work groups, steering committees, or task forces, when the problem is solved, they disappear. These collaborative groups have great potential for putting together recommendations that positively impact the organization. At the same time, they provide fertile ground for the playing out of departmental rivalries and turf wars over priorities and resources.

Accidental Matrix

We call this (Figure 5.3) the accidental matrix because it grows out of a situation that was not part of a plan.

Again, there are many instances of accidental matrices that occur. In one example, I was retained by a major financial services organization to help develop a customer service program for one of the major divisions. Five weeks after beginning work on the program, it accidentally came to light that three other divisions in the organization were engaged in virtually the same activity. With some minor variations, the core competencies that were being addressed were the same in all cases. The inescapable fact was that it made sense for everyone working on this problem to work together rather than suffering the costs of redundancy and other problems caused by a lack of standardization.

Anyone who has worked for a long period of time in a large organization has examples such as this. Perhaps another way to look at the accidental matrix is that it should have been a planned matrix to start with. However, in highly structured functional organizations, this type of redundancy is almost always inevitable. Waiting for this type of cross-functional collaboration to take place on its own can be very damaging to the organization.

Figure 5.3
Accidental Matrix

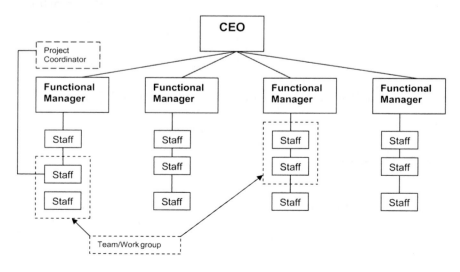

Here are some places to look for matrix opportunities that might not exist.

- Any company-wide initiative mandated from top management creates the potential for redundant responses.
- Rapid expansion of the organization or a new acquisition. In the latter case, redundancies can be inherited. While most of these redundancies will be revealed during the due diligence process, the resolution of the redundancies is often done in a non-collaborative way. This leads to poor performance and low morale in both the acquiring and the target companies.
- Separate technical departments searching for a similar solution but using different technology miss opportunities for effective collaboration.

Spontaneous Matrix

This form that we are calling a spontaneous matrix could also be called a "managers' matrix" (Figure 5.4).

While it is possible that staff members at all levels might find themselves in circumstances where it becomes obvious that working together cross-functionally will provide the best solution for everyone's needs, it is most likely that this connection will happen at the functional managers' level. Functional managers have the greatest opportunities to collaborate cross-functionally because in most organizations they periodically meet and interact with each other. When a group of functional managers is confronted with an issue that affects several of them, there is motivation for them to collaborate on a solution.

Whether or not a spontaneous matrix occurs depends a great deal on the climate created by the executive to whom the functional managers report.

Figure 5.4
Spontaneous Matrix

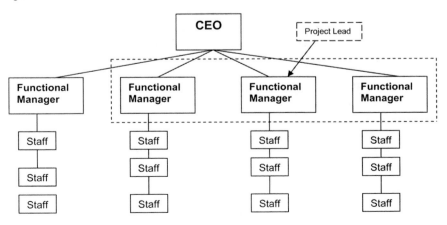

Executives who are successful in creating a collaborative environment project positive feelings about their managers' ability to collaborate effectively and solve common problems. Rather than positioning themselves as great problem solvers, they position themselves as facilitators who can provide input to help the management group meet its goals.[7]

A by-product of successful collaboration between functional managers could be the dissemination of this process down through the ranks. Experience has shown that this will not happen by itself. However, any successful matrix management begins with a significant and meaningful buy-in by the functional managers involved.

The software project mentioned earlier in this book is an example of how effective a spontaneous matrix can be. The Reuters executive who was responsible for making it happen had just taken over the team and brought with her a much more collaborative approach than the group had known previously. Even though it was the first time that functional managers from each of the key areas involved in the development, marketing, and administration of this important piece of software were in the room at the same time, the climate that was created enabled them to build significant trust and perceive the advantages of working together to meet a difficult deadline.

Isolated Matrix

The isolated matrix shown in Figure 5.5 could also be called a "task force," "special project team," or any of several other names that indicate a group that has been established to meet specific objectives outside of the mainstream.

The classic example of the isolated matrix is the "Skunk Works" formed in 1943 at Lockheed Aircraft Corporation. There is much to be learned about effective team operation from the way the Skunk Works was set up and led by its founder Clarence L. "Kelly" Johnson. However, the example of how it operated in isolation is the important point here. Charged with developing the first U.S.-built jet aircraft, XP-80, Kelly and his group of engineers demanded and were provided an unprecedented opportunity to work outside of conventional organizational approaches. Among his "fourteen rules," Kelly listed several that related to the effectiveness of isolation.

- The Skunk Works manager must be delegated practically complete control of his program in all aspects.
- The number of people having any connection with the project must be restricted.
- Access by outsiders to the project and its personnel must be strictly controlled by appropriate security measures.

These tenets and others relating to cost, inspections, and reporting enabled the Skunk Works to design, develop, and deliver engineering technology of

Figure 5.5
Isolated Matrix

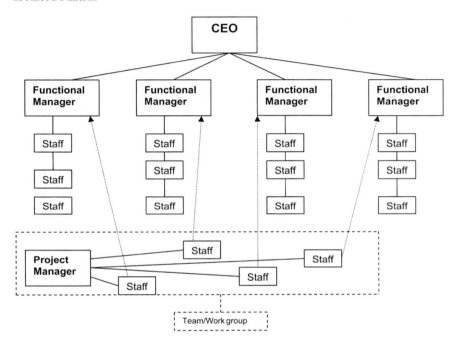

high quality in record time. While there are plenty of success stories for isolated matrix teams, there are just as many if not more examples of where they have not been effective. In most cases where isolated matrix initiatives produced disappointing results, the cause can be traced back to a lack of independence provided to the project manager or other types of interference on the part of functional managers trying to assert control over the outcome of the project.

Informal Matrix

In hierarchical functional organizations, it is not uncommon to find most employees interacting almost exclusively with other people in their functional areas. However, for a variety of reasons, there are always individuals in an organization who strive to make contact outside of their functional boundaries. Figure 5.6 illustrates an informal matrix. They establish relationships with others in the organization for several reasons. They may require information or resources that are not available locally. They may be strategically making these connections in order to enhance their influence in the broader organization. They could be joining activities outside of the mainstream of the business for social enhancement.

Figure 5.6
Informal Matrix

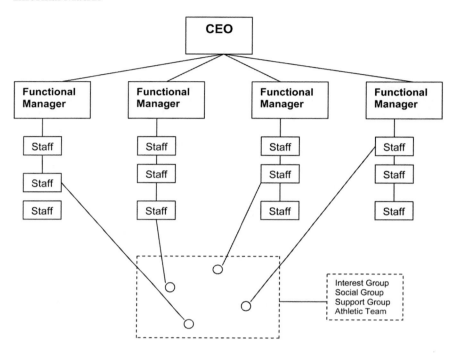

These efforts toward making connections outside of the immediate corporate neighborhood create an informal network that can play a large role in the way information is processed throughout the organization.

Using informal networks is a powerful strategy for managers who want to gain more control over their environment through exerting influence. Establishing new communication relationships in the organization can provide a manager with a broader perspective and enable him or her to influence how needs are prioritized and decisions are made that affect his or her performance. The more highly structured an organization is, the more powerful informal networks are as a source of information. An informal network that spans functional units is a matrix. These personal networks can be of two types: radial and interlocking. A radial network occurs when a person interacts with selected people in the organization who do not necessarily interact with each other. An interlocking personal network occurs when all members of the network interact. Interlocking networks are generally found within the functional areas since they require a great deal of contact, and the individuals involved are generally similar to one another in function, interests, and so forth.

Radial networks provide the main opportunity for matrix involvement, since members of this network tend to come from various parts of the organization. Most organizations have some form of informal matrix. Places to look for them would be interest groups, social groups, support groups, and athletic teams among others. A major by-product of the informal matrix is relationship-building. The informal matrix plays a large role in this regard. The day-to-day pace of events combined with the increasing need for information works against the relationship side of the equation in any organization. Managers and others who participate in the informal matrix opportunities build better business relationships, receive more feedback about what is going on, and are presented with fewer surprises that create major problems.[8]

MAPPING THE ORGANIZATIONAL MATRICES

Making decisions about matrix management begins with understanding where they already exist. Because of the current reluctance to discuss matrix forms by using the term matrix management, it is necessary to reconceptualize the cross-functional activities that are already taking place in the organization. Table 5.2 below provides an opportunity to take an inventory of where the matrices in an organization currently exist. This matrix map is also a good springboard for a focus group activity with cross-functional members.

This simple diagnostic will help define how cross-functional activity is influencing the culture of the organization. Ask some of these questions:

- If we were to look for various types of matrices in your organization, where would they be found? At what levels in the organization? Associated with which product lines and services?

- Who participates in these matrix activities? Are there more representatives from some functional areas than others? Are there functional areas of the organization that are conspicuous because of their nonparticipation in cross-functional activities?

- Can you provide specific examples of where cross-functional activity is adding value to the organization or where impediments to these activities are inhibiting success?

- Which matrix types seem to be most prevalent? Is most of your matrix activity accidental or is there a concerted effort to employ cross-functional resources?

Table 5.2
Matrix Map

Matrix Type	Where Located	Member's Functional Areas	Example
Planned			
Accidental			
Spontaneous			
Isolated			
Informal			

These questions lead toward an understanding of the type and level of matrix activity in the organization. The next step is to make an assessment of how effective these forms are in helping meet organizational goals.

In the next chapter, we will be examining the role of leadership in harnessing existing matrices and developing new potential through cross-functional involvement. For those who take the lead in this initiative, we will be examining various factors in the organization that can be positively impacted by effective leadership.

CHAPTER 6

The Changing Face of Leadership

Leadership is inspiring an organization with a vision of the heights it can accomplish, and engaging people at all levels in the challenge to achieve high-level results. Too many managers have been seduced by the quick fix; squandering effort, time, and resources without gaining any competitive advantage.

—Michael Tull[1]

Today's economic realities have placed extreme pressures on traditional organizations. Globalization and other environmental changes are causing organizations to adopt modes of communication that quickly disseminate information for adaptive decision-making. Functional organizations cannot respond effectively to these pressures; therefore, informal communication networks, decentralized matrix structures, and participatory decision-making make organizations more effective at adapting to the turbulent environment. In addition to the external pressures, organizations are also feeling internal pressures because of the new demands and individual needs of their employees. These challenges call for a different type of leadership. Managers and supervisors are being called upon to adapt their approaches in order to offset these internal pressures.

CONTINGENCY THEORY

We have discussed contemporary theory previously in the context of how organizations respond to changing environments. Here, we look at how contingencies can dictate management behavior. Most research points to the fact that a leader who provides some structure appears to be the most effective at accomplishing productivity and employee satisfaction. However, leadership needs to be adaptive for the same reasons that the organization needs to be adaptive. When serious changes such as a shift to a matrix structure are introduced in the environment, this adaptation is forced because of contingent factors such as cultural values that affect how much structure and control a particular group seems to need.

Almost at the same time that matrix management began to develop as an organizational form, several contingency theories came into being. These leadership approaches acknowledge that there are several factors including members, skills, experience, cultural values, the actual tasks of the group, and the time available to achieve those tasks that affect the type of leadership likely to be effective.

Leading cross-functional teams heightens the effect of contingencies on the potential outcomes. Having to adapt leadership style and substance to the ever-changing contingencies supports my contention in previous writing that leaders need to become facilitators. Leaders who are effective at managing contingencies, including those presented by matrix management, incorporate several of the tenets of the various contingency theories. First of all, in their facilitative role, successful leaders exhibit four specific behaviors.

1. They provide sufficient information and have the ability to process and handle a large amount of information.
2. They adapt to the needs of the group they are leading by taking on a variety of functions needed within the group including task and maintenance roles.
3. They help group members make sense of decisions and actions performed within the organization by supplying an acceptable rationale.
4. They focus on the here and now and stop the group from jumping to unwarranted conclusions or adopting stock answers too quickly.

In addition to these functional behaviors, they need to adapt to factors dictated by their relationship with the team and their position with regards to legitimate power over the group. For example, a project manager leading a balanced matrix team needs to employ a different set of behaviors than a project manager leading a team in a project matrix environment.

Many of the qualities that we associate with leadership are not easily discernable. Early studies on leadership behavior pointed out that leadership was a set of shifting traits that adjust to contingencies.[2] Too many leadership theories presented today subscribe to the "Do it my way" philosophy. Or, so and so must be a great leader because his or her company experienced momentary success. When we examine the competencies for effective leadership in today's environment, seven factors stand out.

1. Effective leaders are active communicators who can express their ideas clearly and concisely; they speak clearly and fluently; and they have a facility in verbalizing problems, goals, values, ideas, and solutions.

2. Effective leaders communicate the group's vision and mission. Perhaps more than anything else, the way they communicate reveals an extensive knowledge about the issues and an understanding of the procedures that facilitate accomplishment.

3. Effective leaders are skilled in coordinating the information and ideas of others. They have good analytic skills and apply critical thinking that leads to a thorough evaluation and integration of the information they receive. They provide structure to unorganized information, ask probing questions to bring out pertinent information, and help others focus on activities relevant to the overall goal.

4. Effective leaders own their opinions but express them provisionally. They suspend judgment and encourage full consideration of minority viewpoints. They tend to withhold their own opinions about the actions to be taken until they have heard the offerings of others. By reserving judgment, these leaders are perceived as being open-minded.

5. Effective leaders appear to be group centered. Successful leaders articulate the vision and the mission in such a way as to inspire a desire for an eventual commitment to the accomplishment of the goals and objectives. Furthermore, their personal commitment is clear to all, and they are willing to confront individuals who appear more self-centered than group centered.

6. Effective leaders demonstrate respect for others. They are sensitive to nonverbal signals and the feeling these signify. They perceive the needs and goals of individual members and adjust behaviors to these needs. They also display common courtesy.

7. Effective leaders share in the success of the organization. Although leadership carries with it the temptation to take credit for the accomplishments of the group, effective leaders share as equals both within the group and when dealing with outsiders. They credit people for their accomplishments and work with individuals to develop their leadership competencies. They are good at expressing appreciation.[3]

Leadership needs to be exerted at all levels of the organization. While many of the competencies listed above are appropriate for both top and middle managers, organizational leaders with positional power have other obligations regarding the matrix as well. First of all, decisions need to be made whether the use of the matrix approach is the best solution for whatever challenges the organization is facing. If the matrices in your organization have evolved on their own in response to some felt need, a decision needs to be made as to whether these matrices will be supported or abandoned and replaced with a more effective means of achieving the necessary end.

In some companies, only one or perhaps a few divisions may benefit from the formally established project-driven matrix. It is possible for matrix forms and more functional forms to exist successfully side by side assuming that top leadership understands what it's doing in this regard and has the situation under control. In most companies, it has become virtually impossible to develop a single organizational chart that realistically portrays the maze of relationships that exist within that organization.

Experience with matrix design has shown that when a matrix is being implemented in the early stages, it will create a disconnect between the behavioral reality and the structural form. Where leadership has failed in the past is that it has mandated the structural design changes but failed to take a series of critical actions that need to be initiated and monitored. Moving from a traditional hierarchical organization to a matrix will inevitably create conflict. Superior–subordinate relationships become blurred, and levels of responsibility and authority become confused and require clarification. Being a leader in a matrix transformation requires patience because changing an existing design to a fully functioning matrix could take several years. It must be continually supported and reinforced to ensure that all the people in the organization understand and accept the multiple authority and responsibility patterns that exist.

For the most part, the quality and character of leadership are inextricably tied to the group or entity being led. Though difficult to define, elements of leadership need to be discovered, internalized, and practiced by anyone who would aspire to managing groups of any size. Although at any moment, shifting contingencies may require different types of leadership, there are perhaps three things about leadership that are universal.

UNIVERSAL CHARACTERISTICS OF LEADERSHIP

There Is a Felt Need for Leadership

In most situations where human beings congregate, there is a felt need for leadership. This need for leadership can be seen throughout the full range of reasons that groups form. Informal social groups require leadership in many of the same ways as groups that are formed to combat some real or perceived threat. Fashion leaders tell us what to wear; opinion leaders tell us what to think.

Leadership Is Emergent

Put any group of people together and give them a task, and within a relatively short period of time they will naturally divide themselves into roles, and one of those roles will be leadership. Leadership emergence has been associated with a number of different characteristics. Some research points to the fact that emergent leaders usually are selected by elimination during a two-stage process. At first all members have potential to become the group's primary leader. However, during the first stage, those members who appear quiet, uninformed, or dogmatic are rejected by the others. In the second stage, people who try to lead in an authoritarian or manipulative manner are eliminated. Finally, the person most skilled in verbalizing ideas emerges as the leader by the consensus of the group.[4]

Other recent studies of leadership have pointed to other characteristics that are associated with leadership emergence. One of these is termed *self-monitoring*, which refers to a person's abilities to monitor both social cues and their own actions in a given situation. High self-monitors are sensitive to contextual cues, are socially perceptive, and are able to respond flexibly according to what seems needed at any given time.

Leadership Is Stable

A third factor about leadership is stability. Once a leader has been identified, groups are very reluctant to make leadership changes, even when they have determined that the leadership is less than optimal. These factors may seem at times to be in conflict with the ever-changing dynamics of the organization. However, if a weak designated leader has been in place for any significant period of time, the organization has made adjustments to compensate for the lack of leadership competency. In fact, others in the organization such as a functional manager who feels empowered by filling a leadership vacuum at the project management level will be threatened by the advent of new leadership.

In a matrix configuration, the overall system of the organization and the subsystems are continually under pressure from the environment to adopt modes of communication that allow the individual units to quickly disseminate and receive information in order to make the most informed decisions. Leadership plays a significant role in how information flows in the organization. Strong stable leadership requires an understanding of both the formal and the informal communication channels in the organization, and the ability to apply techniques and strategies for influencing that communication.

LEADERSHIP IN CONTEXT

When we examine some of the characteristics of effectively functioning cross-functional groups, one of the characteristics that stands out is a clear definition of group members' relationships with one another. Or to put it another way, the roles that each member plays in the process of working through the tasks the group has been assigned. The concept of leadership carries with it a mystique that tends to obscure the more earthbound fact that it is one of many group roles that can be played by several individuals depending on the needs of the group at any given time. It is useful to identify the various roles that occur in group activity. Several approaches to role classification have been attempted and put forth over the last half century; however, the most enduring and widely accepted classification is the one developed by Kenneth Benne and Paul Sheats.[5] Despite the fact that their classification of roles was originally published in 1948, the Benne and Sheats classification is still widely accepted and used in the textbooks on group communication. In fact, more recent studies verify the current usefulness of this classification model.

The model breaks group roles down into three types: task roles, maintenance roles, and dysfunctional roles. Understanding that all classification systems may oversimplify the situation by asserting that individuals will adhere to one role or another during the group interaction process, the model is useful in identifying what the specific role behaviors are. During the course of any group interaction, various individuals may take on different role behaviors. However, when this is looked at in detail, we usually discover that despite the variances most people tend toward prevailing roles based on the context within which they are participants.

- Task roles
  Task roles relate to the task output of the group. They focus on the business of moving the action forward toward a conclusion, a decision, or a solution.
- Social and maintenance roles
  Maintenance roles affect the interpersonal dynamics of the group. They have a strong influence on climate.
- Dysfunctional roles
  Dysfunctional roles refer to those behaviors that are primarily self-centered and impede the progress of the group.

THE LEADER'S ROLE

One of the intriguing things about this taxonomy is that the role of leader is not listed in any of the categories. That omission says more about what leadership is than had it been included as a category on its own. Leadership behaviors incorporate several of the roles listed as task roles, at least a few of the social and maintenance roles, and none of the dysfunctional roles.

For example, one might expect a leader to be an initiator, an information seeker, and in some cases an information giver. Certainly, leaders seek and give opinions and take on a clarifying and coordinating role. Good leaders also energize their groups and certainly provide evaluation and criticism of the group product. The primary social and maintenance roles that a leader might take on include being a supporter and encourager, a harmonizer when it is called for, and a gatekeeper to make sure that the groups are not stymied in their efforts to accomplish their tasks. When we attempt to articulate the role of the leader, we can see that it incorporates the potential for many different behaviors. The most successful leaders are those who have the span of understanding and the flexibility to move between various role behaviors as the need for them becomes recognized.

Effective project leadership in the matrix environment poses an additional challenge. Project managers need to function as leaders while they are facilitating the task activities with their direct reports. However, beyond the task of conducting or facilitating effective meetings with their teams and other managers, those who would aspire to be recognized as organizational leaders need to project some qualities beyond simple role assimilation. These qualities can be grouped in three categories that I call the three Cs: consistency, commitment, and courage.

ORGANIZATIONAL LEADERS ARE CONSISTENT

Being consistent is not just a matter of doing the same things over and over. Consistency begins with developing a common vision that organizational members can understand and adhere to. It is a point of view about what the organization does and the manner in which business is conducted that underlies and influences all of the activities of organizational members. A climate of consistency provides clear direction and priorities, clarifies roles and responsibilities, responds to a set of core values that relate to all aspects of doing business, and remains relatively stable regardless of other changes occurring in the organizational system.

By and large, people tend to follow those who operate with a vision of where they are going. This vision must be accessible and appear unshakable. Some leaders generate this vision from within and then disseminate it to the people around them. Others work with their people to create a common vision. Regardless of how the vision is acquired, its presence will focus the direction and align the energy and resources of the organization to achieve the desired goals.

Successful project managers tie their personal vision with the vision of the larger organization. They work with their team members to identify the mission and goals of the team, out of which come the roles and responsibilities of each individual.

In addition to articulating a mission and setting a vision, project managers need to communicate direction and priorities to their people. When team members are clear about the organizational priorities, they are able to make appropriate decisions about which issues to tackle and in which order.

Once the vision has been articulated and the mission statement completed, meetings are set with each team member to explore individual goals and objectives. Managers should clearly indicate their priorities and be prepared to negotiate and make adjustments based on input from the staff. Holding periodic update meetings to review the group's progress against the goals that were set is a good follow-up. One way of managing those meetings effectively and providing your team members with a feeling of empowerment is to shift the agenda responsibility from one member to another for each of the meetings going forward. In this way, each subgroup has the feeling that they are being provided with an opportunity to get their issues on the agenda.

CLARIFY ROLES AND RESPONSIBILITIES

Another major factor with consistency is being clear about the roles and responsibilities of the group as a whole as well as of the individuals in that group. Clear delineation of responsibilities builds ownership. Also, because of the nature of change, it will be necessary to continually revisit and, in some cases, reshuffle roles and responsibilities. This clarification is an ongoing process in a dynamic organization. Open and frank discussion about differences in role expectations among team members should be encouraged. In order to be perceived as a strong leader, in those instances where consensus is not possible or appropriate, the project manager needs to make a decision and let the team know the rationale for that decision.

MARKET THE MISSION

A consistent leader dedicates effort toward presenting the group's mission to the larger organization. Not only should managers be primary spokespeople for the efforts and achievements for organizations, they should also select people from within the team ranks to represent the group's point of view through presentations to other groups in the organization.

FOCUS ON PERSONAL AND PROFESSIONAL DEVELOPMENT

Consistency is also demonstrated through a project manager's focus on the personal and professional development of the people, including training and providing access to both internal and external resources to raise competency levels and job satisfaction. This often requires direct contact and, perhaps, negotiation with the various functional managers who are responsible for providing this kind of support. This also serves to carry the message and priorities of the team to the full organization. It enables the setting of consistent standards and allows the people in the organization to feel comfortable about being on the right track. When the opportunities arise to provide individual coaching, the project manager's interactions with the team members should have a future focus rather than being merely evaluative. When criticism is warranted, it should be consistent with the standards that have been clearly communicated to the individual in question.

COMMITMENT

Managing across functions requires a leadership approach that depends more on influence than on giving orders. A major factor in the amount of influence a project manager exerts within his or her team and beyond is the recognition of the project manager's commitment to particular issues and points of view. Successful leaders command attention. They demonstrate an eagerness to present their points of view. They are firm and direct when stating expectations or confronting issues or ideas that run contrary to their established thinking. Some managers confuse assertiveness with aggressiveness. The simple difference is that while both behaviors have confrontational elements, assertiveness focuses on the issue, whereas aggressiveness attacks the individual. Commitment is also demonstrated by the rapidity of the response to issues. Effective managers address concerns as soon as possible. Delaying response, even for the best of reasons, can often be interpreted as a lack of commitment.

COMMUNICATING COMMITMENT

Commitment is shown through clarifying and communicating the vision. The clearer and more compelling the vision, the easier it is for others to understand and endorse it. Commitment is also demonstrated through enthusiasm. The more excited and energetic managers are about meeting their goals, the more committed others are likely to be in supporting it. Enthusiasm is displayed by conveying how important the goals are and how pleased you are that people are willing to pitch in and work with you.

Managing cross-functional teams provides an excellent opportunity for managers to demonstrate their commitment and to have an impact on a large number of people. They state their opinions forcefully and don't hesitate to voice their thoughts or label them as their own.

Commitment is also demonstrated through interactions with the management above. When a manager recognizes that a decision from upper management might have a negative impact on his or her team, it is dealt with directly and clearly by presenting upper management with the impact the decision will have by citing tangible consequences. If it is necessary to make concessions, they should be positioned as being important to the larger organization. People's trust in their manager is enhanced when the manager's motives appear directed at benefiting the entire organization.

COMMITMENT TO TEAMWORK

Commitment is shown not only through adherence to issues and positions in the organization but also through a demonstration of the manager's commitment to the group and teamwork in general. As the leader, a manager's actions and policies affect the overall ability of the group to work together. The most effective project managers

- Create structures that are conducive to both work groups and teams.
- Encourage and reward cooperation rather than competition between different work units.
- Provide the means for groups to communicate their goals and objectives to one another and ensure that they are mutually supportive.
- Provide subgroups with the authority to act upon their decisions.
- Set an example by demonstrating group leadership as well as being an effective group member.

- Acknowledge and celebrate work group and team accomplishments.

These actions not only demonstrate a commitment to this process but also keep the motivation and momentum going.

ORGANIZATIONAL LEADERS ARE COURAGEOUS

Today's environment demands that leaders make decisions that involve risk and take a stand in the face of ambiguity or conflict. Successful leaders confront problems directly and take action based on what they believe is right. As a result, they win the respect and commitment of others by standing up for what they believe and making the tough decisions. They also stand behind their people who take risks and make difficult decisions. Taking risks in any situation requires conviction, if a particular action is going against the mainstream or is not widely accepted. And yet it is often the willingness of an individual to take risks that stands out most when he or she is being evaluated as a leader.

WHAT IS IMPORTANT TO YOU?

Ask yourself what is really important to you, what is worth fighting or standing up for? Think about the legacy you want to leave your organization, what things or qualities you want to be remembered for. Identifying what is most important to you establishes the foundation for leading courageously when it matters. Look for situations in which others may be overly concerned about taking a stand, but where you strongly believe in the correctness of your position based on your convictions and your understanding of the situation. This is an opportunity to develop a rationale and make your position clear to others. Rather than waiting for these opportunities to come to you, you need to actively look for opportunities to stand up for what you believe.

TAKE ACTION

Managers are often faced with situations in which taking the most appropriate course of action carries with it a backlash of complaints, problems, and negative reactions. Successful leaders will not avoid taking action in these situations; they confront the tough issues head-on, since they understand that in the long run no one benefits by ignoring issues that must be addressed and resolved. In fact, more respect and concern is shown for people when tough issues are confronted rather than ignored. Obviously managers want to choose their battles carefully, since they can't possibly do everything. But it is especially critical for them to address the issues that get in the way of their mission.

It is often a good idea to enlist the input from the team regarding the areas most important for taking risks. When important individual or team issues are brought to attention, it is critical for a project manager to respond quickly. Indecisiveness may result in the perception that the manager cannot make the tough choices or take a stand on issues. Some managers are concerned that taking a stand on a particular issue will cause others to dislike them. Even the most popular leaders are not liked by everyone, but even if a person is not liked, his or her ideas may be valued. Consistently seeking approval projects to others that a manager lacks confidence. Risk-taking is discussed openly with direct reports: (1) Model the behavior for them, (2) Talk through the problems, and (3) Describe how you arrived at the decision you chose.

EMBRACE CHANGE

Perhaps one of the most courageous actions a leader can take is to embrace change. The willingness and ability to champion change will go a long way toward determining anyone's effectiveness as a manager in today's competitive business environment. Successful change efforts require the commitment and support of key individuals throughout the organization to plan, manage, and implement the change. Managers need to develop a strategy to get the necessary people on board. In some cases, this will require courage, since there are risks involved in suggesting change actions.

Meetings need to be held with each person individually to explain the rationale for the change, the potential benefits, and the implementation plans. To maximize buy-in and minimize resistance, managers need to involve others in this process. When employees feel that they are valued participants in planning and implementing the change, they are more likely to be motivated toward successful completion. Solicit and use the input from the team, peers, and upper management when planning any change effort. If the change means significant loss for some individuals or areas of the organization, don't downplay the message and pretend that it is anything other than what it is. Just deliver the message including the support that will be provided during the transition period. Be straightforward and honest about the implications of the change.

Beyond just perceiving the need for a change in ongoing processes and procedures, successful leaders reach beyond their everyday assignments and responsibilities and identify new initiatives and improvements within the organization. They create clear and compelling visions of the changes that are necessary. They identify the people who can help make the change a reality, and they take the initiative for sharing their ideas, conclusions, and reasons for excitement and commitment with others.

LEADING FROM A DISTANCE

Managing virtual work groups, or even traditional groups that have interactions with virtual participants, creates challenges for management that are both similar and unique in a traditional setting. The basic qualities of leadership already described here are applicable to groups that may be fully or partially dispersed and have little or no opportunity to meet face to face.

Difficulty of scheduling, timing, work interaction, and general communication can be significantly magnified in the virtual or remote situation. A leader's ability to be effective under these conditions requires confident and deliberate actions to keep people on track. A key to effectively leading in this manner is to get to know the members of the team as much as possible. What are their needs and concerns? Their level of technical expertise? The level of supervision they need to feel comfortable? Also an effective leader will select the combinations of technology best suited to the needs of both the project and the participants.

Another key is to limit the expectations and objectives for each virtual session to segments of a problem or issue that can be dealt with in the time available. For all its supposed efficiency, electronic interaction takes much more time to accomplish the same ends as a face-to-face meeting. Despite the drawbacks, virtual groups are an essential part of today's working world. Leading in this environment emphasizes the need for building trust, creating a feeling of community, setting clear objectives, praising individual success, coaching as needed, and finding opportunities for the group to interact in ways that will enable them to see one another as human beings.

Leadership in today's complex and ever-changing organizations is not for everyone. The old adage that "it's lonely at the top" has never been truer than it is today. In my role as an executive coach, I often find that the executive's greatest need at times is to just have someone to talk to and share with. Much is expected of today's leaders:

- They have to be individual contributors in a significant way.
- They have to be effective communicators.
- They have to balance toughness and compassion.
- They have to be accessible without being overwhelmed.
- They have to be energetic and driving without bringing too much stress to others.
- They need to appear courageous, committed, and consistent to those who report to them and to those to whom they report.

The role of the project manager takes center stage in the implementation of any type of matrix. It could be argued that even informal matrices require that someone assumes the responsibility of leadership in order that the network can survive. The next chapter takes a closer look at the project manager as a leader—more specifically, a leader of people not tasks and deliverables.

CHAPTER 7

The Project Manager as Leader

It's a beautiful summer evening. Your backyard is full of friends, family, and neighbors. Giant glowing balls hang from trees and candles, lanterns, and twinkle lights bathe the lawn in amber. There's soft Italian music, long tables of food, bottles of wine, and tubs of icy beer, soda, and French water.

Then your cell phone rings. Your date squints one eye at you as if saying, "Don't you dare answer that phone." You wink and answer anyway—you have to, you're the project manager.

Yeah, you're the freakin' project manager.

—Joseph Phillips[1]

Project management is the cornerstone of any matrix design. While the role of the project manager increased in complexity as well as authority, as we move along the continuum from a functional matrix to a full project matrix organization, the underlying assumptions and requirements of project management remain the same. Most people reading this book will have a better than fundamental knowledge of project management. There are many good resources available that provide detailed techniques and strategies as well as methods and tools for use in effective project management. As such, our discussion here will focus more on the high-level understanding of the project manager's role in meeting his or her objectives within the matrix framework.

In recent history, evolving matrix structures gave rise to four types of project managers: project expeditors, project coordinators, matrix managers, and pure project managers. The four types of project managers were defined largely by the structure of the parent organization and the principal purpose they served. The implications derived from these four models influence the authority possessed by each of the four types of project managers and the control that each exerts over the various types of project resources including the project team members.[2]

Galbraith (1971), whom we have discussed before as a progenitor of matrix management theory, further examined the intricacies of the matrix organization and his continuum of project management structures: the functional matrix, the balanced matrix, and the project matrix. The continuum was anchored on each end by the functional organization and the project team, respectively. Along the continuum from the functional organization to the project team, the relative degree of authority and control exerted by the functional managers decreases and shifts to the project managers. There are challenges that confront project managers to varying degrees in each of these three project management structures. These challenges include,

1. Power struggles as boundaries of authority and responsibility overlap,
2. Conflict, especially with respect to the use of shared resources,
3. The integration required to coordinate work across projects, and
4. The challenge of securing team member motivation and commitment to project outcomes.[3]

The truth and durability of these stated challenges have been proven over time. Nearly every failure to implement a successful matrix can be traced to a failure to recognize or mitigate these issues.

We have already discussed some of the potential pitfalls of matrix management. The need for increased communication and negotiation between the various elements in the organization requires that managers and staff work effectively between and among themselves. The matrix creates many opportunities for conflicting directives, uncoordinated activities, territorial battles, professional jealousies, interpersonal strife, role ambiguities, and many more dysfunctional behaviors. It is the hope that top management in the organization has provided insight and support for the significant cultural change brought on by a shift toward matrix management.

Even so, the ambiguities created by this design raise serious concerns among the people who have to live with it. More often than not these concerns are personal rather than objective. Individuals engaged in projects within a matrix form have questions about their career development: "which teams should I belong to?," "how to identify the important goals and successes of the total enterprise?," and perhaps most importantly, "how do I know whether I am doing a good job?" Most definitions of project management define the role as being responsible for project results, the accomplishment of project objectives on time and within budget. These factors are certainly at the heart of what the project manager must accomplish. However, project mangers more often find themselves dealing with the human elements in the project than on the timing or workflow of the group's tasks and responsibilities.

TYPES OF PROJECT LEADERSHIP

Some contemporary views of team structures provide a useful construct within which to examine project leadership. More recently, researchers in the new product development domain have adopted team structures called the functional team, the lightweight team, the heavyweight team, and the autonomous team.[4] The functional team in this model does not have a designated project manager. This can be viewed as a type of "weak matrix" that we have discussed earlier. The experts residing in each of the participating functional departments are responsible for the work within their domain. In some cases, the work passes from one function to the next as the project progresses through the life cycle. The lightweight team structure introduces the lightweight project manager, who is considered light in two important ways.

First, the lightweight project manager is typically a junior or middle level manager who possesses little status or influence in the organization. His or her activities are generally confined to maintenance roles such as scheduling and arranging venues. Second, the lightweight project manager does not possess authority or control over the key members of the project team who continue to work within their functional organizations. By contrast, the heavyweight project managers are typically senior managers within the organization who have primary influence over those assigned to the project team and supervise their work directly. However, the team members in this model are not permanently assigned to the project. As such, they continue to rely on the functional manager for matters related to career development.

I'm not sure that what is termed as a "lightweight" project manager is necessarily a person who lacks status or influence in the organization. I am more comfortable with the notion that "weight" is determined by the level of interest. I can imagine situations where very high-status people could be placed in roles as lightweight project managers, perhaps as an oversight function.

Finally, there is the autonomous team, which is also led by a heavyweight project manager. The description of the autonomous team mirrors closely the project team we have discussed earlier. In the autonomous team model, the individuals are formally assigned, dedicated, and collocated to the project team. The project leader possesses complete control over project resources. The challenges differ between lightweight and heavyweight project managers. Whereas lightweight project managers primarily facilitate the activities of the project team, heavyweight project managers must lead the team and champion project causes. These responsibilities demand a more active leadership approach that includes regular interactions with project team members to ensure that project decisions are made and implemented in a timely fashion.

While the structure of the parent organization plays a significant role in defining the structure of the project team models and the corresponding authority, responsibility, and control entrusted to the project manager, there are several additional factors that may exert a strong influence on the structure of the project team and introduce unique challenges and leadership implications. With the recent advances in communication technologies and the rise of the global economy, many project teams include team members who are geographically dispersed and exhibit greater degrees of diversity. This diversity may be due to cultural differences, or it may simply result from the varied skills, educational levels, personalities, and unique interests of the individual team members. Regardless of the source of diversity, the contemporary project management environment presents many challenges to the project leader.

A study done by Grant, Graham, and Heberling (2001) looked at project team models developed from thirty-two detailed case studies written by graduate students enrolled in a project management course at the Air Force Institute of Technology in Dayton, Ohio. Each student conducted a structured interview with the project manager of an actual defense-related project. The structured interviews incorporated questions on project planning, scheduling, budgeting, contracting, and software support. As part of the interview, each project manager was asked to estimate the percent of work time each team member dedicated to the project. The results of these interviews were documented in formal case study reports. The analysis of these reports yielded four project team models.

The thirty-two case studies analyzed included the development and implementation of information systems, the design and demonstration of technology prototypes, and the development, production, or modification of defense systems and equipment. The parent organizations that sustained each of these projects included project organizations, functional organizations, and matrix organizations. Finally, the thirty-two case studies included projects at all stages of the project life cycle.

This was a very ambitious and comprehensive study. Although there are probably too many variables that influence the outcome, the results are quite interesting. Once again, the researchers show a propensity for making up creative names for the same phenomena.

THE PROJECT TEAM MODELS

The study presents four project team leadership models: conductor leadership model, champion leadership model, choreographer leadership model, and club director leadership model. The degree of involvement on the part of the project manager (heavy or light) and the team members (heavy or light) determined the specific project team model. These metaphors have interesting connections with the reality they are being compared to. But it does make me wonder if the research team consisted of a musician, a dancer, and a maitre d'.

Conductor Leadership Model (Heavy Project Manager–Heavy Project Team)

The analogy used here is a musical conductor. In the conductor leadership model, the project leader and the core team members dedicate nearly all of their time to the project. Like the conductor, when it comes—time to perform—the project manager is integrally involved, often directing the contributions of individual team members. And like the orchestra, all team members participate throughout the performance, working in concert with the project manager and complementing the contributions of fellow teammates.

The study showed that the conductor model was the most prevalent project team model in the thirty-two case studies. This model was most frequently associated with parent organizations that were structured as project organizations or as project matrix organizations. Specifically, the case studies revealed that several projects managed under the auspices of ADPOs (Advanced Development Program Offices) and "basket" SPOs (System Program Offices) were best represented by the conductor leadership model.

There are several team leadership challenges associated with the conductor leadership model. Many of these can be directly linked to the increased demands of managing a full complement of dedicated team members. Attention to team selection becomes more important. Working in a team with many dedicated teammates increases the opportunity for role conflicts or interpersonal conflicts. Additionally, team priorities may become unclear as the team members impose priorities based on personal interests or are influenced by the priorities of a functional discipline. Finally, as opportunities to communicate increase, opportunities to "miscommunicate" also increase.

Grant, Graham, and Heberling reported that the most frequently identified team leadership implication of the conductor leadership model was the importance of staffing the team with the best people. Team selection activities were identified in two-thirds of the conductor leadership model case studies. Selecting compatible and collaborative team members appears to be particularly important for these teams because all of the team members and the project manager will work together almost constantly for the duration of the project. The relatively high degree of team interaction and collaboration suggests that project team performance can be highly influenced by paying increased attention to the skills and compatibility of the project team members during the team selection process.

While clearly in agreement that team selection is a high priority in project matrix teams, I fail to see the hierarchy of importance. Surely any team needs to recruit the right people to meet the objectives regardless of the degree of involvement of the project leader.

Another interesting implication observed with the conductor leadership model was the cross training of disciplines, which resulted from the frequent interactions of team members. As each team member learned more about each other's roles, they became better able to address each other's concerns while performing their primary functions. They also developed the ability to compensate for absent teammates, at least occasionally. This is a key point, and it is too bad that when it happens it is often accidental. Well-functioning teams need to consciously facilitate the transfer of knowledge and understanding between participants as part of a process strategy.

Finally, the conductor leadership model facilitates frequent communication between members. The conspicuous team identity and frequent interactions between team members provide an environment that is very conducive to interpersonal communication. Also, the case studies indicated that most of the project managers conducted team meetings on a weekly basis. These regular meetings provided a forum to address team problems and issues, review team plans and progress, and reward team successes.

Champion Leadership Model (Heavy Project Manager–Light Project Team)

In this model, the project manager dedicates nearly all of his or her time to the project, but the team members support the project only when specific support is required. Consequently, the success of the project rests squarely on the shoulders of the project manager. In practice, the project manager may have the dedicated support of one or two core team members to help move the project forward. The remaining team members contribute to the project performance on an "as needed" basis over time as project requirements dictate. For example, a test manager may become very involved as the project test phase approaches, and then withdraw after testing is complete.

The champion leadership model occurred in a wide variety of parent organizations. These projects included several ad hoc teams formed when an individual was tasked to complete a project that required the support of several organizations. These projects were managed under the auspices of project organizations, matrix organizations, and functional organizations. The primary determinants for the champion model appeared to be the scope and duration of the effort, rather than the nature of the parent organizations. Generally, the projects were given the assignment of a full-time manager; however, the scope or duration did not warrant the assignment of a fully dedicated project team.

The challenge for the project manager in the champion leadership model is to gain commitment for contributions from team members who dedicate only a small portion of their time to the project. These projects must always compete for team member involvement against a host of alternative priorities. The sometimes infrequent interaction of team members may lead to project instability.

The champion leadership model presented some unique implications. Several full-time project managers sought team member commitment by engaging the supervisors of the team members, rather than dealing directly with the team members. These project managers were more interested in cultivating the support of the functional supervisors so they could count on receiving quality support in the right amounts at the right times. It seems the enduring relationships at the heart of several of the examples of the champion leadership model were between the project manager and the senior managers of the divisions that supported the project. This approach directly secured team member commitment, and it also helped to reduce the number of conflicting priorities since the team member supervisors sponsored the team member involvement. The study also noted that this strategy was conducted in concert with efforts to build team cohesiveness and unity.

Choreographer Leadership Model (Light Project Manager–Heavy Project Team)

In this model, the project manager plays a key role in project activities, such as organizing and planning the efforts the team will perform, but dedicates a majority of his or her time and effort to multiple projects or different activities. The team members in this model are the real performers. For the team members, the project consumes a majority of their time, effort, and concentration.

The choreographer leadership model existed in two scenarios. The first was in a government project office that did not possess the human resources to staff the project. Consequently, the project manager contracted with a technical assistance contractor to obtain the necessary resources. In this arrangement, the technical support contractors comprise the project team working in support of a government project manager who has several additional projects to manage.

The choreographer leadership model also occurred in the multiple project environment, which is typical in large matrix organizations. Specifically, there were cases when the project manager working in a project office of a large matrix organization was responsible for several projects. The number and scope of competing projects precluded the project manager from dedicating a majority of his or her time to the project. Yet the project required the full support of the functional offices within the program office. The researchers note that the choreographer leadership model was the least prevalent model observed in the sample of thirty-two projects.

I would comment that this factor of prevalence reported in this study needs to be read as contextual; that is, in other work environments, there would be different results. For example, in management consulting the typical model aligns a project officer who is responsible for many projects with a subordinate who may also be responsible for more than one project. However, a project manager is assigned specific responsibility for one project.

Three barriers to team development and leadership arise with the choreographer leadership model. First, the credibility of the project manager may be jeopardized due to the relatively small amount of time he or she dedicates to the project. As the team members dedicate the majority of their time to the project, they will become the project experts. They will derive the direct experiential benefits that accrue from active project involvement. The gap in project knowledge and awareness between the project manager and the project team will grow over time. Ultimately, this imbalance may handicap the project manager and place his or her credibility in doubt. Competition for team leadership may also develop as team members attempt to compensate for the diminished involvement of the project manager. Moreover, direct competition with the project manager may result if the team members' leadership expectations go unfilled. Finally, team member commitment may also wane over time. Team members may conclude that if the project is not important enough to warrant the full involvement of the project manager, then it certainly does not warrant their full commitment either.

The study revealed some key implications for leadership. A review of the case studies revealed a leadership approach that appeared to overcome the challenges of part-time project management. One project manager assumed a very firm and authoritative leadership posture with the team members. While not always active in project performance, the project manager made a concerted effort to monitor team progress and to directly confront team members whenever performance varied from expectations. The team members were aware the project manager was monitoring their performance and that they would be held directly and immediately accountable for any mistakes or problems they created. Consequently, the team members in this case internalized the challenge of avoiding the confrontations associated with unsatisfactory performance. The project manager created the illusion of omnipresence and rewarded exceptional performance. A second strategy, which was successfully used, was to appoint a deputy manager or an acting project manager who fulfilled many of the team's expectations for leadership in the project manager's absence.

Team member commitment may be especially fragile when the project manager contracts outside of the parent organization for the support of the team members. If the project manager views team commitment as a contractual imperative rather than an attribute of a high-performance team, he or she may neglect to conduct team-building activities across contractual lines that may well result in improved project performance.

Club Director Leadership Model (Light Project Manager–Light Project Team)

This model depicts a situation in which all project participants, including the project manager, dedicate only a limited portion of their time to the specific project. Like a club director, this project manager is responsible for a wide variety of events that need to be organized, planned, directed, and controlled. And like the members of the club, the project team members will participate in some but not all of the activities and events. In the club director leadership model, all of the team members may recognize the importance of the project, but each faces competing priorities and opportunities.

This team leadership model occurred frequently in functional organizations and in large matrix organizations. Within the functional organization, the formation of interdisciplinary project teams is often complicated by the degree of specialization in each functional area. Project participation falls victim to the prevailing functional priorities. Likewise, in a large matrix organization, a small or relatively low-priority project is unlikely to receive the commitment of a full-time project manager or project team. The project will be accomplished, but only after the project team members satisfy higher priorities and first assume that managers are setting organizational priorities as a guide to the application of resources to those endeavors that are most important. Project leadership and team building in this environment should remain consistent with organizational priorities.

The primary challenge to leadership of a team that conforms to the club director leadership model is the lack of team definition. A majority of the case studies describing these teams noted the lack of a defined team structure. Additionally, the relatively low priority of these projects frequently prevented the project from receiving the full support of senior leaders, and the project had low member involvement, conflicting priorities, low team member commitment, and inadequate communication.

The researchers felt that one approach that would be well suited to the club director leadership model would be to formalize team member commitments at the very beginning of the project. There are a variety of formal mechanisms available to secure team member commitments, such as linear responsibility charts like the RASIC, the assignment of discrete work packages, and memoranda of agreement.

A very interesting trend in the patterns of communication between members of the team appeared in the case studies. Excessive communication by the project manager on a club director team can have very negative impacts on team member interest and commitment. Meetings that run too long, or cover too wide a variety of topics, can have a negative impact on meeting attendance and will decrease project performance. Successful project managers will be very selective when inviting or requiring team members to participate in meetings. He or she needs to balance the desire for team identity and communication with the cost in commitment that results from the perception that time spent in meetings is time wasted and that the project does not merit the investment in time required. This is potentially a source of team members feeling overworked that we discussed in Chapter 2. Another justification for including this study in our exploration of existing matrices is that in many ways the findings mirror the observations in Chapter 5 relating to planned matrix, accidental matrix, spontaneous matrix, isolated matrix, and informal matrix.

Despite the important differences highlighted in the study just discussed, there are some universal attributes of project leadership that cut across the divides suggested in the four models. Project teams are made up of interdependent roles. When information hoarding, blame seeking, and self-protection kick in, a breakdown isn't far behind. Sue Dyer (2006), author of "Partner Your Project," writing for the newsletter *Projects at Work*, provides five concepts to help create a foundation that allows for cooperative relationships and teamwork to grow.[5]

Take Ownership of Problems

When a problem occurs, if your first reaction is "I thought Bob was supposed to do this" or "I paid a lot of money to get this right" or "These numbers are just wrong," then the next logical step is to figure out who is to blame for the problem. Most of us are very skilled at analyzing who is to blame. Meanwhile, no one is addressing the problem that you've uncovered. When blame seeking starts, all communication between team members stops. And if it takes for the team two days, two weeks, or two months to begin to talk about the "real" problem, that time can never be recaptured. It is lost forever. This is a huge risk to the success of the project.

Blame seeking is indicative of a process problem in the team. There is a lack of trust either in the leadership or in the motives or in the competencies of the other team members. Pointing fingers is a clear sign that the group is not acting as a collective, and individuals have not bought in to the primacy of the success of the team over individual motives.

It doesn't matter who created the problem. What does matter is that everyone understands and resolves the problem quickly so the project (or team) is not damaged. So ownership of problems means that everyone owns the problems and seeks solutions, not blame.

Commit to Full Disclosure

The project manager needs to tell everyone everything that he or she knows. How can the team possibly create plans or know where the inherent problems are if it doesn't have the best information? Many times team members hold their cards close to their vests, not revealing everything that they know. They think that this somehow gives them an advantage. But, in fact, when you are working on a project (or on a team) you are interdependent—you need each other in order to succeed. Controlling information, causing the other team members to not make the best decisions or plans, really impacts the potential success of your project or initiative.

Honestly discussing all problems up front can help assure success. Problems occurring after the project is underway have a greater impact than problems identified and worked out during the planning phase. So at the very start of a project or initiative, take time for the team members to share what each sees as potential problems. Then you will have time to mitigate the impacts. Full disclosure means you tell everyone everything that you know—the good, the bad, and the ugly.

As part of the process of team development, discussion and activities should be focused on team concerns. As a project manager, what are your concerns? What do you feel will provide obstacles for the team's success? These same questions should be answered by every member of the team.

Empower Others

Team members often get frustrated when they aren't allowed to make the decisions that they feel are critical for a successful project. Even worse is when someone higher in the organization overturns a decision they've made. Pushing the power and decision-making down to the project/team level is critical for the success of the project or initiative. Project managers don't need to make all of the decisions. You will generally get better quality decisions from those closest to the issues.

In many organizations, power resides away from the project and the team members don't feel that they can make decisions. Good project mangers employ courage to confront the organization and empower the team to do whatever they feel is required in order to succeed. Many teams are doomed before they start. Empowering others means you negotiate the decision-making down to the project level before you start. This often means "managing up"—getting agreement from superiors or stakeholders that they will respect the results and decisions of the team. It is hard to proceed with confidence unless you have these assurances.

Partnering Requires Commitment

Partnership doesn't just happen by itself, it takes commitment to build and grow. There will be many things along the way that cause team conflict. The project manager cannot be conflict averse. Issues need to be confronted directly. There will be times when it would be easier to just walk away instead of sitting down face-to-face to work things out. That is not an option. The best commitment you can make is to tell each other the truth and then deal with it constructively.

If there are legal agreements between you as partners, don't let them solely define your working relationship. The judicial process is adversarial by design. This can undermine the ability to build the partnering relationships required to succeed. You can't be both "partners" and "adversaries." Commitment means doing whatever is necessary to keep your partnership alive and well.

Build Trust

Trust is the keystone of partnership. Your partnership will be as good as your ability to create and grow trust between your team members. It allows for open, honest communication. The project manager needs to model trust behavior for the team. Your first interaction sets the tone for the relationship. If you go into the relationship trusting and seeking to cooperate and work together, then you are highly likely to get that attitude in return. If you go into the relationship trying to protect your interests and unwilling to be open, that is probably what you will get in return. Game theory shows that cooperative relationships produce larger wins than those where participants are protective and self-serving.

For a team, "fairness" is the underpinning of creating trust. It is when someone feels that something is "unfair" that trust begins to erode. When you have a problem or issue, always put "fairness" on the table and discuss it first. What is a fair way to resolve the issue? Most teams can figure it out. Measure the level of trust on your project and you will have a good idea of how successful your project will be.

I suggest meeting privately with each of the team members before the project begins and on a regular basis throughout. Don't be afraid to ask process questions like "How do you think it's going?," "What can I do better to make your job easier?," and "Where do you see problems in the relationships between team members?"

DEVELOPING A SENSE OF COMMUNITY

The previous guidelines and others like them address the all-important issue of team development and team maintenance. However, in the matrix environment, team success is inextricably tied to system components beyond the immediate confines of the team. Some current writers and observers of the project management scene have taken hold of the idea of "project community," a concept that asks the project leader and the team to look beyond their artificial boundaries for the collaboration and support needed for project success. Talking about his own realization about community, David Schmaltz puts it this way:

The change didn't happen overnight. It started as no more than a hint, a whisper, really, and most who heard this whisper translated it into their same old dialect. The concept was, like it is now, called "project community," but most experienced "team" members heard this phrase as nothing more than a new age way of saying "project team," which, of course, didn't result in anything other than adding another...buzzword to an already richly buzzword-infected vocabulary....

When the change finally started kicking in, I didn't notice it at first because it didn't exhibit itself in any observable behavior. The first subtle shift was an almost imperceptible erosion of what I later learned to call my Us/Them Boundary. Rather than think of my "team" as "us" and the rest of the organization as "them," I found myself increasingly unable to exclude from "us" more of those who had previously fallen outside my sphere of interest because they were so obviously outside my sphere of formal influence.[6]

As a way of defining the idea of community more specifically, start with the common language that describes the key components of project management. We use the term "team" to describe the group selected or compiled to do a task. But inherent in the word "team" is the notion of competition.

Teams are set up to beat other teams, not cooperate with them. Proponents of the project community approach claim that *team* induces a separateness, a sense of "us against them," which subtly includes some while excluding everyone else; you're either on the team or not.

Of course, this is not startling news. Anyone who has studied even a little bit about group process can understand this exclusivity or "groupness" as part of the human condition. Project community asks the project manager to look beyond the natural boundaries, to examine and face the underlying causes of old and continuing failures, to stop repeating approaches that don't work, to level with other members of the organizational community about just how very disappointing the working relationships had been, and to choose to make them different.

At the outset of a project, the project manager would be well served to begin with these questions.

1. What are the outer boundaries of the project community? The community consists of all people both inside and outside the defined project membership who are in some way affected by the project. The key is just to identify and understand the needs of the community, not develop a comprehensive plan to provide satisfaction of everyone's needs. Simply addressing personal goals in the community will help each person find a reason to support the effort and engage in the success of the project.

2. What level of investment should be expected from each member of the community? Not everyone in the community needs to be committed to the project's objectives. Probably only a select handful is needed to make the emotional investment required of full commitment.

   While experimenting with the community approach with an organization trying to move from a passive repository of work provided by the whim of the customers to a more entrepreneurial business development culture, we identified a community that consisted of forty-one people. The first task was to get a clear picture of the core competencies the organization had to offer to the marketplace. The members of this group were then allowed to self-select themselves into one of these three categories based on their level of interest, time, etc.:

   • Level 1 (Core Team)
     Hands-on development of the core competencies and associated presentation to the managers.

   • Level 2 (Advisory Group)
     Advisors to the team who could be consulted on drafts or generally comment on the team's output. This also provided a buffer for people who weren't selected for the Core Team for various reasons, but had expressed a high level of interest.

   • Level 3 (Resource Group)
     Resource providers who could be called on to provide specific information about their area for inclusion in the competency statements.
     Some individuals better served themselves and the project by maintaining a compliant relationship with the effort, simply agreeing to follow directions. Others would find community in extending empathy, while some helped by

objecting, resisting, or maintaining a deliberate indifference to the outcome. Schmaltz speaks of a project manager at Oracle Corporation who was asked how he would ensure his project's success given the chaotic internal environment. He replied that he would work hard to ensure that Larry Ellison wouldn't be interested in the effort. Larry would be a member of the community, but his role, his project within this project, would be fully satisfied if he found insufficient interest in it to get actively involved. The project manager noted that projects seemed to operate more chaotically whenever Larry took a personal interest in the outcome, and his best strategy for ensuring smooth sailing was to engineer the captain's indifference.[7]

3. What are some reasonable expectations? Sometimes the project manager's expectations can get in the way of creating robust matrix communities. By insisting that everyone be committed to an effort, we potentially undermine the community's best attempts to adapt. Commanding commitment (if even possible) from everyone in the organization will lead to unsatisfying results. Threat and obligation may create compliance, but satisfying someone else's goals is not a high motivator for most people. When we step back and consider our own expectations in light of real-world self-interests, we easily conclude that our innocent attempts to create a fully committed effort undermine our best intentions. What do I want? What have I got? What will I settle for? Answering these three questions can create an unexpected portrait of a really robust community.[8]

It should be apparent that most of the research and suggested actions presented in this chapter deal with relationship issues. In my experience, when a project falters or fails completely, it is more often because the project manager was unable to manage the dynamics of relationships both inside and outside the team. In Chapter 8, we will look at communication style as a key component for project management success.

CHAPTER 8

Communication Style in Project Management

How do you eat an elephant? One bite at a time. The same is true for any project. According to the Project Management Institute (PMI) there are five process groups and nine knowledge areas that make up the crux of project management. There is a vast body of generally accepted practices, tools, and techniques available within the profession of project management. Any project management methodology is replete with things like activity duration estimation, cost budgeting, critical path method, Gantt chart, or work breakdown structure—mainly focusing on the left-brain functions. This structured approach is enormously beneficial for project managers to get their arms around a project and guide it to a successful conclusion.

But oftentimes what is lost in the shuffle are softer, "big picture" aspects of project management that are typically associated with the right brain. Why are they important? Because there are very few projects that are purely technical in nature. Virtually every project is "of the people, by the people, for the people." And people happen to have feelings, imaginations, beliefs and a sense of present and future. If you look at projects that have failed to meet the expectations, more often than not either ignoring or underestimating this reality was probably responsible for the undoing of the project.

—Abhay Padgaonkar[1]

The central concept of most project management processes is control. As such, organizations continually strive for attainment of an automated ideal. However, this approach usually fails due to the fact that the fundamental building block of successful collaboration is quality human relationships.

A key component for building quality relationships with a team is an understanding of the role of a style.

Style can be characterized in two different ways. First, it can be observed as a communication style of an individual who aspires to leadership. On this basis, style relates to verbal and nonverbal behaviors that contribute to the leader's total effect. The second way to look at leadership style describes style as an approach to leadership. This style dimension is determined by the pattern of behaviors that a particular individual uses when applying leadership.

Research into the effect of style on the emergence of leadership has pointed out that group members whose communication was perceived as quiet, tentative, or vague were viewed as uncommitted to the group and not knowledgeable about the group's task. Those who exhibited these behaviors were quickly eliminated as potential leaders because it was felt that they did not contribute ideas or help organize the group. In the change environment created by the introduction of a matrix, or in an existing matrix, the resulting ambiguity calls for strong direct leadership. Those who did emerge as leaders made more attempts to suggest procedures for the group and thus helped get the group organized. In addition, their participation profiles were high in maintenance roles like contributing to procedural issues and also fairly high in task roles like information giving and seeking but were low in stating opinions.[2]

There has been a tendency to think of biological gender as being a determinant of group leadership. Males were perceived to more likely emerge as leaders than females. However, more recently, gender has been a much less important factor, and recent studies find no significant differences in the amount of communication style behaviors contributed by men or women. In these studies, it appears that the type of task did not influence the emergence of leadership, but that group members' individual abilities to contribute to the task and their commitment to the group goal regardless of sex were associated with their emergence as leaders.

Despite the fact that leadership is contextual, that is a person may be perceived as a leader in one situation and not in another, it seems equally clear that people with the ability to adapt their behaviors and who possess communication skills that help clarify the group's task and motivate other members will exert influence on groups. Through careful self-monitoring, project managers who aspire to be perceived as leaders will identify the needs of the particular group and be flexible enough to adapt to those needs.

STYLE APPROACHES

The classical description of leadership approaches included three basic styles:

1. *Democratic leadership*, which encouraged members to participate in group decisions including policy-making decisions.

2. *Laissez-faire leadership*, which takes almost no initiative for structuring a group, but is responsive to inquiries from members.

3. *Autocratic leadership*, which exerts tight control over the group including making assignments, directing all verbal interaction, and giving orders.

Autocratic and democratic styles of leadership correspond closely with the *Theory X* and *Theory Y* assumptions about human beings described by management theorist Douglas McGregor.[3] Theory X assumes that people don't like to work and must therefore be compelled by a strong, controlling leader who supervises their work closely. Theory Y makes a different assumption: people work as naturally as they play and are creative problem solvers who like to take charge of their own work. Leaders who accept the assumption of Theory Y behave democratically by providing only as much structure as the group needs and by allowing members to participate fully in decision-making and other aspects of the group's work. Research on these two approaches has been relatively consistent. The democratically led groups are generally more satisfied than the autocratically led groups, and most people in Western culture prefer democratic groups. Other findings show that autocratic groups tend to work harder in the presence of the leader, but they also experience more incidents of aggressiveness and apathy. Comparison between democratic groups and laissez-faire groups shows that groups perform better with some structure and coordination, particularly with regard to problem solving. Although leadership that provides some structure appears to be the most desirable for both productivity and satisfaction, there are contingent factors such as cultural values that affect how much structure and control a particular group seems to need.

CONTINGENCY THEORIES AND LEADERSHIP STYLE

These contingent factors have given rise to contingency theories or approaches relating to leadership. These approaches acknowledge that there are several factors, including members, skills, experience, cultural values, the actual tasks of the group, and the time available to achieve those tasks, that affect the type of leadership likely to be effective. The selection of how a leader may structure a particular meeting is dependent upon the same contingent factors that we take into account for the larger group. It is not necessary to provide an exhaustive discussion of the various contingency approaches in order to identify those issues that are most germane for a manager to develop leadership style. However, a brief summary is useful as a jumping-off place for listing these attributes.

The Functions Approach

Functional approaches attempt to define specific behaviors to be performed by leaders. Without naming leadership, the work of Benne and Sheats discussed earlier in chapter 6 falls into this category. B. Aubrey Fisher sorts through the task and maintenance roles and identifies four functions performed by leaders.

1. Providing sufficient information and having the ability to process and handle a large amount of information.
2. Enacting a variety of functions needed within the group (e.g., task and maintenance roles).
3. Helping group members make sense of decisions and actions performed within the organization by supplying acceptable rationale.
4. Focusing on the here and now and stopping the group from jumping to unwarranted conclusions or adopting stock answers too quickly.[4]

Fiedler's Contingency Model

Another theorist, Fred Fiedler, takes a somewhat different view. Rather than seeing leadership as a relatively open and adaptable behavior, he views leaders as people who are relatively inflexible. The leadership behaviors are preferred by the individual and are used more effectively than other selective behaviors. Fiedler's contingency model concludes that there are three factors upon which appropriate leader behaviors are contingent:

1. The relationship between the leader and the people being led.
2. The structure of the task or the responsibilities of the group.
3. The leader's position in terms of legitimate power over the group.[5]

In Fiedler's view, there are certain individual characteristics that make people suited for leadership only in certain types of contingencies, so it is more productive to match prospective leaders to situations than to try to change the individual style. However, this suggests that the tasks and responsibilities of the group will remain relatively stable. This may have been more the case in 1967 when Fiedler's book was written. In today's environment of rampant reorganization, it is not uncommon for an individual who is designated as a leader because of his or her executive position in the organization to find himself or herself responsible for a wide variety of suborganizations within a relatively short period of time.

Hersey and Blanchard's Situational Model

The widely accepted situational leadership model developed by Hersey and Blanchard moves in the opposite direction. They believe that people are flexible enough to adapt their behavior to meet the needs of many groups. The most effective leaders, in their view, are able to assess both the relationship issues and the task orientation associated with applying leadership strategies. Not only does the leader need to adjust to the overall needs of the group, he or she also has to have the ability to adapt to the needs of the members of the group at all points during the life of the group. It assumes a deep knowledge and understanding of each individual's needs and competencies. Hersey and Blanchard provide a very useful construct for small group leadership; however, it becomes unwieldy for leaders of large organizations to attempt to understand everyone in the organization at that level.[6]

The Communication Competency Approach

The communication competency model grew out of the felt need to account for contingencies without overwhelming the leader with complexity. The approach is the result of work done on small group leadership, but many of the principles that derive from the competency approach are applicable to leaders of large organizations as well. The communication competency model is based on the assumptions that leadership involves behaviors that help a group overcome obstacles to achieving their goals and that leadership occurs through the process of communication. It is a contingency approach, because it assumes that the actual context facing the leader and the group is constantly shifting so that different competencies may be needed at different points.

The key factor with all the contingency approaches appears to be flexibility. Regardless of the stimulus for adapting to varying conditions, contingency theory underscores the fact that effective leadership requires a sensitivity to the process as well as the substance of accomplishing a set of objectives. What may work with one set of contingencies or one group of people may not be appropriate in all situations.

INFLUENCING TEAM BEHAVIOR

In the matrix environment, much of the project manager's work depends on his or her ability to influence members of the team who are not immediately under his or her control. Each team member potentially brings a combination of personality, mind-set, motive, and a personal agenda. Having a specific strategy for influencing teams can mean the difference between success and failure.

Project managers who are good influencers have a good set of communication behaviors and know how and when to use them. They have a clear understanding of their own preferred communication style and are adept at discerning the style of others. They strategize which style to use based on their assessment and the result they want. They are flexible in developing an approach and responding in the moment. They are flexible to some degree with regard to the style that they can employ in a given situation.

How one develops his or her style profile goes well beyond the boundaries of this book. However, psychologists tell us that style is the relationship between a number of potential response factors in the personality, ranging from our need to be competitive, to be accommodating, to collaborate with others in certain circumstances, and in other circumstances to avoid issues that are unpleasant to us.

Although our core self-concepts are relatively unshakable and unchanging, in our moment-to-moment interactions with the world we are able to draw on various aspects of this mix of available responses to assure that what we are presenting to the world is appropriate for the given situation that we're in. However, it has been demonstrated through the use of testing instruments that most of us present a fairly consistent predominant style when interacting with others.

Several instruments are on the market for use by human resources professionals and corporate training personnel that are designed to help individuals discover their predominant styles. Myers Briggs and Wilson Learning Systems are two of the better-known purveyors of such materials, and many organizations have used these inventories as part of management development and other corporate leadership programs.

Another excellent and much less complex instrument is the *Thomas-Kilmann Conflict Mode Instrument (TKI)* published by Xicom in Tuxedo, New York. This instrument grew out of the work of Kenneth W. Thomas and Ralph H. Kilmann. It is designed to assess an individual's behavior in situations in which the concerns of two people seem to be incompatible.

The *TKI* is a self-directed test using a series of thirty forced-choice questions pertaining to conflict situations. The individual selects the most appropriate answer from each pair and then tabulates and graphs their scores. This determines their primary and alternative styles of handling conflict. These are displayed across five "conflict-handling" modes as "competing," "collaborating," "compromising," "avoiding," and "accommodating."

Since originally published in 1974, over two million copies of the *TKI* have been printed. The instrument's original validity study was based on the responses of 339 practicing middle and upper level managers.[7]

The branch of psychology most concerned with style issues is the psychology of individual differences, or ID psychology. The concern of ID psychologists is the study of things which distinguish one person from another. It focuses on those traits and characteristics which point to why everyone doesn't act the same. Sex, age, education, occupation, socioeconomic level, intelligence, and many other characteristics are the items studied by the ID psychologist.

One of the variables, of course, is personality, and—although elusive—it is the most potent one. Style, to some extent, can be seen as the outward manifestation of a specific personality. Because each person's personality is somewhat different, this helps explain why—from a style perspective—we tend to respond to situations in totally different ways. When personalities and the resulting prevailing styles of two or more individuals are in conflict, this can create stress and further affect, alter, or moderate the interactions between the people involved. It is possible that the effect may be to intensify the relationship, as in the old saying, "opposites attract." On the other hand, such conflict is just as likely to weaken a relationship. These style conflicts can have a serious negative effect on your ability to influence.

There are innumerable style traits, which hold the potential for both attraction and repulsion among individuals. All people have dimensions of personality, which serve to increase, or decrease, the stress they experience in a particular situation compared to the stress someone without those same characteristics would experience.

If you are the type of person who is always punctual, you are inevitably going to experience greater amounts of frustration with regard to appointments than people who are more casual about being on time. Moreover, you will have a tendency to react negatively on an interpersonal basis to people who do not share your value for punctuality.

While style differences can be very powerful determinants of how people interact and to what degree one has influence over the other, what we are talking about is a prevailing style. The same personality construct that provides for our differences also provides for our similarities. Any style inventory you select and administer to yourself will demonstrate that, while you have a prevailing style, you also contain within your basic personality some measure of the other available styles.

Our prevailing style emerges much in the same way as other personality factors. When we are very young, for whatever reason, certain behaviors are rewarded while others are ignored or punished. So, over time, we learn that we are most successful using a particular mode of behavior when we interact with the world and others.

Periodically, circumstances cause us to reach inside of ourselves for a style of behavior that differs from our usual choice. While this may produce a measure of discomfort, the fact is that most of us are capable of sustaining alternative styles for some period of time when it benefits us to do so. Where we get into trouble—and why this is so important in the area of influence—is that, unless we focus our attention on the need to reach for different styles in various kinds of interaction situations, we will automatically migrate to our prevailing style, which may or may not be appropriate for the given circumstance.

Jerome D. Frank in his classic work on psychotherapy, called *Persuasion and Healing*, focuses on the relationship between style and influence and the problems that arise from the reciprocal nature of human transactions. When you interact with someone else with some degree of frequency over time, one person's behavior tends to "train" the others to respond in such a way as to confirm your expectations. He cites as an example a paranoid patient who is convinced that everyone hates him, and, because of his surly, suspicious manner, antagonizes other people who originally bore him no ill will. However, the resulting reaction he receives confirms the patient's belief that everyone dislikes him, intensifying his dislike-creating behavior.[8]

In this way, according to Frank, in the psychiatric construct, patients tend to get caught in "self-fulfilling prophecies," and their behavior is both self-perpetuating and self-defeating.

Frank then goes on to discuss more directly the forces of influence that practicing psychotherapists have available to them.

To oversimplify vastly, the two major sources of interpersonal influence are individuals on whom a person feels dependent and those whom he perceives to be like himself. The former, first represented by his parents, later by teachers, bosses, and so on, gain their power through their direct control of his well-being. The sources of influence of the latter—his friends and colleagues—are not so apparent, but probably spring in part from the fact that their attitudes of acceptance or rejection determine his sense of group belonging.[9]

In his book, *Influence: The Psychology of Persuasion*, Robert B. Cialdini supports this notion in another way. Following a discussion about the way in which attractive people in our society reap certain benefits, Cialdini talks about some of the other factors that enhance a person's influence.

One of those factors is similarity.

We like people who are similar to us. This fact seems to hold true whether the similarity is in the area of opinions, personality traits, background, or life-style. Consequently, those who wish to be liked in order to increase our compliance, can accomplish that purpose by appearing similar to us in any of a wide variety of ways.[10]

Cialdini provides us with some examples, including the way we dress. He discusses one study, done in the early 1970s, when young people tended to dress either in "hippie" or in "straight" fashion. The researchers running the experiment dressed either as hippies or as straight people, and asked college students on campus for a dime to make a phone call. "When the experimenter was dressed in the same way as the student the request was granted in more than two thirds of the instances; but when the student and the requester were dissimilarly dressed, the dime was provided less than half the time."

In the matrix environment, the major task of the project manager is to convince members of the project community and, often, the organization as a whole that the needs of the project must be assigned a high priority. In a functional matrix, for example, the project manager is continually negotiating with the functional manager for resources. If good collaboration is not established, the inevitable result is conflict. When this conflict becomes entrenched, it can only be resolved by escalating the issue to a higher level of the organization, thereby diminishing the potential that might have been derived from the matrix approach.

Failure to influence and negotiate effectively leads to a general cynicism toward matrix management in the broader organization. Or, as Michael

Schrage puts it, "[M]atrix management guarantees that top managers must step in to resolve the very conflicts and disputes guaranteed by the organizational design."[11] There is no doubt that matrix structures give rise to the potential for conflict. This is not always a bad thing. Conflict can be healthy and productive if the parties to the conflict are working from a base of collaboration. While style is not the only determinant for collaboration, it is an often overlooked powerful contributor.

CATEGORIZING INFLUENCE STYLES

For any of this to make sense, you first have to accept that we all have a prevailing style. That not being the case, you're better served by moving on to Chapter 9. Most of us, however, have been tested often enough, or presented with outcomes that clearly relate to a mismatch of personality variables, and have come to accept that we project some kind of affect that is potentially accepted or rejected by others. As a personality variable, style has a broad rage of implications for building relationships. In order to be able to identify the various styles available to most of us, we first need to give them some names. Since TCPI (my company) uses an influencing inventory as part of our organizational diagnostic work, the nomenclature presented below relates to that inventory. The Influencing Style Inventory separates behaviors into four types, which we will call Persuasion, Control, Trust, and Vision.

One implication that is important for anyone who would endeavor to influence others is that each of these styles carries with it a set of communication rules. Persuasives prefer to be communicated with in a different way than Trusts. The term we usually use to describe this phenomenon is "rapport." If we are going to succeed in convincing someone to collaborate with us, we have to develop a connection. If we approach someone with the wrong style, we violate their communication rules, and they automatically begin to reject us. The savvy project manager will adapt his or her style as necessary to establish rapport.

Persuasion

Individuals who exhibit a primary Persuasion style are fundamentally driven by logic, facts, opinions, and ideas. They are assertive in presenting their ideas, proposals, and suggestions, and feel strongly that their approach to the way things should be done is the correct one. They are not afraid to take risks and present their ideas—even as a test of others' reactions. They are highly dependent on evidence and arguments from other sources and tend to be quite good at finding these support materials. They are characterized by a persistent and energetic approach when persuading others.

Persuasives tend to be poor listeners, especially when the person speaking is in disagreement, yet they seem to be astute at picking out what they perceive as weaknesses in the other person's position. Rationality tends to overbalance emotion, and if a Persuasive has real power, he or she will tend to use that power to compel compliance.

When Persuasives are effective, it is usually the result of being highly verbal and articulate and of their willingness and ability to participate very actively in discussions and agreements. Persuasives differ from many of the rest of the styles in the sense that they actually enjoy being involved in arguments, and tend to be generally less conflict-averse than people not sharing their style. Persuasives tend to be found in law firms and legal departments of corporations. They often make excellent salespeople, as well as management consultants.

Many people who migrate toward this style tend to depend too heavily on logic and fact to achieve influence. When Persuasion doesn't work, it is because people do not always approach situations or decisions logically and rationally. If a Persuasive is feeling strongly on the emotional level, continued reliance on the normal Persuasive mode often results in higher levels of overt or covert resistance.

Persuasives tend to be at their best when they also have a measure of Trust in their style dimension. This tends to take some of the edge off the assertiveness and makes the person become more collaborative. They look for solutions to problems that are pragmatic and address the substantive or factual issues at hand, but also concern themselves with building relationships for a long-term payback. They will consult with and ask for the opinions of others who may be functional experts or staff members, and are not afraid to share information with other people. Again, and at their best, Persuasives focus on overcoming a problem, not other people. They are adept at gaining commitment to integrative solutions, where the concerns of all parties can be reconciled.

On the other hand, if Persuasives have a high amount of Control behavior in their style, the result can be very difficult for others to deal with. This combination provides a very strong power orientation, and Persuasives with high Control rarely involve others in the planning process and feel that they must decide and carry out decisions on their own. To do otherwise would be a sign of weakness. There is also a tendency to overcontrol and dominate any conversations and to set the communication rules. Interactions with this type of Persuasive will incorporate a style of pushing, demanding, and making flat assertions.

Control

Individuals with a prevailing style in the Control dimension base their actions and interactions on what they perceive as a solid belief system. On the positive side, Control people balance praise and criticism and ensure that the people they interact with know exactly what they want, expect, or require of them. They set standards and tend to apply these standards consistently in judging behavior and performance. These are the detail people and very often the ones to whom others turn to get work done.

The belief system that a Control person adheres to can derive from several different sources, such as policies and procedures, the rule book (as in the military), religious affiliation, accepted conventions of society, prejudice, or personal preferences based on previous experience.

A key problem for Control people is to make an effective distinction between assertiveness and aggressiveness. Being assertive means defending yourself appropriately by focusing your attention on the issues and arguments in question. Aggressiveness is another way of defending yourself; however, it generally results in direct attacks on the people posing the issues or arguments that are in contention.

Often it is more natural for Control people to overuse criticism at the expense of praise. We all know managers whose idea of providing praise for a job well done is to simply say, "Good job!" while, as soon as something doesn't go as planned, they provide very detailed criticism of everything that went wrong. To be effective in using Control, praise must also be used liberally and provided in a detailed way.

Individuals who have a prevailing Control style tend to be particularly effective when decisive, quick action which has the potential for unpopularity is required, as if in an emergency situation. However, the long-term results and fallout from an application of heavy control may have extremely negative aftereffects. Controls tend not to involve others in the planning process and feel that they must decide and carry out decisions on their own. For some Control people, allowing others to participate in decision-making would be a sign of weakness. High Control people also tend to be surrounded by "yes" people, who have found it unwise to disagree. This tends to block off some potentially important information.

Trust

People with high Trust profiles have a need to involve (and sometimes overinvolve) virtually everyone affected by the outcome of a situation. Their underlying way of interacting with the world depends on consensus. People with a high Trust style profile like working in teams and sharing ideas with others. They tend to be more willing to make concessions when confronted with conflict and put their concern for their relationships ahead of winning or following an unpopular policy. Often they allow, and prefer, others to control the situation, and while this type of orientation will many times produce more creative solutions to problems, a group of high Trust people will spend an inordinate amount of time on relationship-building. As managers, high Trust individuals depend on others to carry out plans and actions and tend not to be as concerned with follow-up and supervision.

Unlike Persuasion and Control, which can be conceived as "push" strategies, Trust tends to pull people in as a means of influence. Effective Trust people are successful at making others that their resources are important to the task at hand, and that time and effort will be put forward in order to gain the valuable contributions of others. Trust people tend to promote an atmosphere of openness and nondefensiveness, and—as facilitators—often succeed in achieving a high level of participation. They are active listeners. They tend to be at ease showing their understanding and appreciation of others' contributions. They tend to be positive and freely give over responsibility and authority to others working on their team.

As an influence style, Trust can be very effective in the right situations, since Trust people create a sense of openness and build relationships on a personal level that they can then draw on later when they need allies. Aside from being a powerful style of influence in and of itself, Trust works very effectively with the other styles and should be cultivated as part of the behavior exhibited in situations requiring influence. One unique aspect of the Trust style is that it is reciprocal. In the process of applying the behaviors associated with Trust, a person leaves himself or herself open to be influenced.

On the negative side, they may take too long to get things done and may overemphasize the relationship at the expense of taking a stand or solving substantive problems. Also, there's a danger of Trust people personalizing any given situation. Some high Trust people have a strong need to be liked, and this makes them ideal targets for others who feel the need to tear them down or manipulate them. As managers, Trust people who are too accommodating may reinforce the perception of low authority and conviction. This can serve to undermine personal impact and credibility. It also diminishes the impact that any valid points that they might make would normally have.

Vision

People with high Vision profiles are focused on the future. While they are generally less concerned about relationships than Trust people, they depend on an emotional connection to have their influential impact. They tend to mobilize the energy and resources of others by tapping into their values, hopes, aspirations, needs, and wants.

High Vision people are adept at using altruistic approaches. They are effective at generating a sense of importance for being part of a group that shares a common purpose. They depend on being able to present ideas effectively; however, unlike Persuasives, their appeal is not primarily to the intellect. Effective Vision people have the ability to get others excited about the future as they perceive it. They have an enthusiasm that is infectious and are often charismatic. Unlike Trust people, they are not looking to build a consensus or to share their ideas with others in the hopes of arriving at a common solution or decision.

When a Vision person enters into an influence situation, he or she has already decided on what the outcome needs to be. The objective is to sell that idea to others to the extent that they will agree to work together to achieve the necessary common goal.

On the negative side, Vision as an influencing style can create difficulties, both on a small and on a large scale. On the world stage, we might say that people like Gandhi and Winston Churchill used a lot of Vision in their persuasive approaches. However, so did Hitler, Mussolini, and Napoleon.

AN IDEAL INFLUENCING PROFILE

If it were possible to create an amalgam of all of the good characteristics of each of the styles, the person possessing this ability would be a powerful influencer—simply based on his or her ability to discern and project the behaviors necessary to open and maintain lines of communication with a wide variety of people. While it may not be practical for most of us to assume that we can achieve such an ideal, it is useful to look at what the behaviors might be. The ideal influencing style would have enough Persuasiveness to be driven to find solutions that are pragmatic and address the substantive or factual issues at hand. At the same time, it would have enough Trust in the profile to demonstrate a concern for building relationships to create long-term allies.

The person with the ideal style would carefully consider who else should be involved in the decision, and share the power and the rewards according to the needs of the situation. He or she would consult with and ask for the opinions of others who may be functional experts or staff members, and would not be afraid to share information with other people. He or she would seriously consider, as the Control people do, the policies and procedures that would be affected by any actions or decisions that they might make, and would respect these rules and adhere to them as long as they remain functional, but would be willing to change or move outside of the rules when they felt those rules were restrictive and did not add value to the situation. They would also have enough Control behavior to be dominant when necessary, but the Control would be focused on overcoming the problem, not the other people. They could temper that strength with the ability to merge insights from different people and gain commitment to integrative solutions when the concerns of all parties can be reconciled.

This combination of Persuasion, Control, Trust, and Vision enables a moderate amount of disagreement or differing opinions on an issue to surface, and, by grappling with these issues, a more constructive and creative examination of available options can be carried out. The following guidelines are intended to help you focus on the relationship-building side of influence, with an emphasis on how your style helps determine your effectiveness.

1. Be aware of your style, and get in the practice of trying to estimate or anticipate the style of others with whom you will be interacting.
2. Seek out feedback—honest, candid, and specific—on your style.

3. During every interpersonal interaction, use the opportunity to try and further clarify the substantive issues and needs of the other party.

4. Try to listen to the underlying implications, and the sometimes nonverbalized needs and agendas, of others.

5. To every extent possible, maintain two-way conversations throughout. Watch for periods of time when either you or the person you're trying to influence clearly seem to be dominating the conversation. If you notice this is the case, take action to break rhythm—whether it be your own dominance or other's.

6. Demonstrate understanding and attentiveness to the needs of the other party. Use reflective statements, paraphrasing, and empathizing, to demonstrate and confirm your understanding of their position. Ask questions about their statements, to show interest and to clarify what they are really after.

7. Demonstrate your ability to be open-minded and to accept reasonable, creative alternatives to the ideas you have.

8. Work toward the creation of a problem-solving, problem-focused environment. Try to minimize emphasis on beginning positions and spend or invest time up front in clarifying the interests of all the people involved.

9. Try to minimize personality involvement in conflicts by focusing on the issues. If you are dealing with a person you genuinely do not like, extra effort must be expended to keep the focus on substantive issues. You don't need to like the people you are working with, but you may be required to continue dealing with them as colleagues.

10. As appropriate, ask for advice regarding alternatives and creative solutions to the issues that you have posed. If suggestions on these issues are offered, recognize and reinforce these contributions, and build upon them wherever possible rather than attempting to discredit the suggestions.

11. Be willing to confront conflict and/or objections directly, but in a constructive fashion. Focus on the substance or impact of the conflict, rather than the personality that may be causing it.

As you come to understand your individual style and how to make use of it to your advantage, you will be increasingly able to interact effectively with colleagues, team members, and others whom you need to influence and to make them into allies.

CHAPTER 9

The Matrix Out of Bounds

The *New Yorker* once ran a cartoon by Peter Steiner of two dogs, with one sitting at a computer keyboard saying to the other, "On the Internet, nobody knows you're a dog." Nobody also knows you're in Uruguay.

A tiny country of three million people, wedged between Brazil and Argentina, Uruguay has come from nowhere to partner with India's biggest technology company, Tata Consultancy Services, to create in just four years one of the largest outsourcing operations in Latin America....

By creating an outsourcing center in Montevideo, Tata could offer its clients its best Indian engineers during India's day (America's night) and its best Uruguayan engineers during America's day (India's night).

Most employees here are Uruguayans, but there are also lots of Indians sent over by Tata. It produces both a culture shock—Montevideo doesn't even have an Indian restaurant—and a cultural cacophony.

The firm runs on strict Tata principles, as if it were in Mumbai, so to see Uruguayans pretending to be Indians serving Americans is quite a scene. Said Rosina Marmion, 27, an Uruguayan manager, "Our customers expect us to behave like Indians—to react the same way."

Also, Latin culture, unlike Indian, is very nonhierarchical. "The Indians were not used to someone who says 'no,'" explained Ricard Zengin, 34, a systems analyst. But eventually, "they understand that you are not saying it to challenge their authority but because you think it can be done better another way....In Latin culture, everything involves a discussion...."

In outsourcing, though, Uruguay has leapt ahead of its neighbors by being the first to understand what could be done—that in today's world having an Indian company led by a Hungarian-Uruguayan servicing

American banks with Montevidean engineers managed by Indian technologists who have learned to eat Uruguayan veggie is just the new normal.

—Thomas L. Friedman[1]

During the course of our discussions in this book, we have periodically pointed to "globalization" as one of the key drivers for the development of matrix structures. This is unquestioningly true. But beyond being a cause for matrix applications, globalization brings with it a whole package of ingredients that challenge our recipe for success.

For many organizations, globalization means expanding their operations to foreign countries—parsing the world into European, Asian, South American, and other geographic divisions. For others globalization may also include the building of alliances with organizations not directly under their control, such as suppliers and, in some cases, even competitors. Many companies no longer just do business in multiple regions or countries, adapting to local market differences. Rather, they are thinking and acting globally and locally—executing integrated strategies and operating in each market in the most effective manner. Whether global or local, strategic alliances present an interesting matrix component.

From a cultural perspective, whether you are operating in a multinational environment or with national organizations with radically different cultures, various steps need to be taken to support the resulting matrix issues. The human resource element is perhaps the most complex challenge. The first order of business is to develop people from "headquarters" who can function effectively in the target country. The more successful companies focus on helping employees to understand and effectively handle cultural requirements by building sensitivity to languages, national customs, legal and regulatory environments, and other country and regional differences.

The question that comes to mind is how companies should adapt the business model and how much to standardize from country to country? Creating ventures in foreign markets requires training on both sides. The home company needs to learn about the employment habits and attitudes in the foreign country as well as the foreign employees need to learn about the habits and attitudes of their new employer. Which system should take precedence in a global venture? Does the home country have the advantage because it is in charge, or does it adapt to fit into the new environment? There are several important steps that managers need to take in order to ensure a successful transition when expanding globally.

- Define the corporate vision and mission statements in the new global environment.
  - Does the current vision and mission apply to different cultures?
  - Is the new global team involved in creating the vision and mission?

- Set objectives and strategies that include the new foreign workforce.
  - Are the current objectives and strategies appropriate in the new culture?
  - Should some strategies be altered if they are not culturally appropriate?

These things will not ensure a successful transition but will create an awareness that some actions may need to change. When a company expands globally, it arrives in the new country on its cultural cruise control. American companies have been known to come into a country and expect everyone to immediately conform to the "American" way. A successful foreign venture requires a look at the habits and customs of the new culture.

There are three basic attitudes that management can take in an international setting.

- Ethnocentric attitude (home country oriented)
  - Viewing the world with domestic references.
  - Managers tend to treat international departments as outlets for dealing with domestic issues.
- Polycentric attitude (host country oriented)
  - Viewing the world with some domestic references.
  - Each national market is looked upon as a unique market requiring a separate, independent, and different strategy.
- Geocentric attitude (world oriented)
  - The company views itself as citizens of the world, not of a particular country.
  - Gradual elimination of the very idea of a home or host country.
  - National borders are ignored, and the world is conceptualized as a single market.[2]

The attitude that managers adopt depends largely on the industry. For example, many IT firms are setting up offices overseas and adopt a more polycentric attitude so they can have a strong base in the local technology markets. IT companies need service and support from the local people if problems arise. Having a strong base in the local market by recognizing the uniqueness and independence of the foreign country allows for greater support from the local community.

IBM is a major case in point. The company boosted its Indian staff from 9,000 at the end of 2003 to 23,000 at the end of 2005, and, according to an internal planning document made public by a union, the total is on its way to 38,000. In another significant move, IBM announced on October 12, 2006, that its global procurement headquarters is moving from Somers, New York, north of New York City, to Shenzhen, China. This is the first time the headquarters of a corporate-wide organization (IBM) has been located outside the United States.[3]

According to the company, the move illustrates a shift underway at IBM from a multinational corporation to a new model—a globally integrated enterprise. "In a multinational model, many functions of a corporation were replicated around the world—but each addressing only its local market," said Chief Procurement Officer John Paterson, who is relocating to China. "In a globally integrated enterprise, for the first time, a company's worldwide capability can be located wherever in the world it makes the most sense, based on the imperatives of economics, expertise and open environments."

IBM has been operating multinationally for a long time, and it has paid a lot of attention to managing cross-border assignments and to matching individual interests, capabilities, and development needs with business requirements and local circumstances. However, with this move the company is giving more attention to the broader strategic challenges of building business that is global and not simply all over the world. "IBM is a global company," Paterson said. "And today that is as much about making efficient and effective use of skills everywhere in the world and integrating them globally to serve clients, as it is about developing deep local relationships in markets around the world. We are becoming a globally integrated company that allows us to do both."

Perhaps following IBM's lead more companies need to develop the mind-set and capabilities among their people so their organizations can extend their influence beyond local and regional boundaries and gain the significant leverage of being global. The most effective companies will pursue long-term commitment, investment, and risk management to achieve results in targeted markets. They will make decisions and implement actions with an understanding of global economics and market potential. They will also help managers and associates understand the global threats and opportunities and engage them in developing effective strategies for addressing them. In his article, "Are We Global Yet?" James Walker (1998) underscores the importance of having personnel relate effectively to matrix management.

We must enable everyone to appreciate (and cope with) the uncertainty and rapid change inherent in global businesses. Rapid globalization requires organizational flexibility. Opportunities develop and pass quickly, requiring organizations to seize them through alliances and partnerships. However, many managers and other key employees still feel more comfortable with traditional ownership and control; they have difficulty working within complex networks or matrix organizations.[4]

As unyielding and entrenched as subcultures of an organization can be even when they are located in the same country, these issues are compounded when matrix forms are applied to distant geographic components. People, problems, and work are located in specific places and need to be managed. A matrix provides the best opportunity for addressing the demands of both local and global realities by focusing management attention on both operating effectively and managing the people. In and of itself, however, the matrix cannot solve the problem. Success depends on managing the points where these two imperatives are reconciled.[5] A well-functioning matrix allows local and global realities to be reconciled. However, when not managed effectively, it allows individual managers to pursue their own narrow global objectives without regard for the local consequences, and vice versa.

The key challenge for global matrix management is loyalty. Most people develop their loyalties locally. They connect more easily with people they see daily, socialize with, and share a clear set of cultural norms with, in terms of both the broader culture and the culture of the local organization. Simply drawing dotted lines on an organization chart to someone in another country doesn't create a working relationship.

As part of a study of international managers conducted by Global Integration, over 2,500 international managers were asked whether their primary loyalty and obligation should be to their local colleagues or the remote (normally central) part of their team. In Spain and France, over 60 percent preferred loyalty to the center; in the UK, Ireland, and China the majority of people (nearly 70% in the case of China) preferred loyalty to local colleagues. One interesting discovery was that HR managers most preferred loyalty to be local.

Other findings showed significant differences between cultures regarding control or autonomy. Functional and industry cultural differences were just as prominent as national cultural differences. Kevin Hall, President of Global Integration, points out some of the challenges of breaking down these barriers to create a team atmosphere.

"In face-to-face organizations it is important to work on relationships and team building, but a lot of this activity comes 'free' over coffee or a beer in the evening. In remote organizations we need to schedule time and effort to make this happen explicitly."[6] Recently, I am discovering managers who actually prefer the virtual team primarily because they can avoid the relationship-building activities.

Because employees in a matrix often receive competing demands on their time from managers more senior than they are, there is a need for a mechanism to escalate and openly challenge competing managers. According to Hall, matrix structures are most successful in cultures where there is relatively low "power distance" between the individuals and their managers—North West Europe, the United States, and Australia. Where management styles have traditionally been more paternalistic or directive (Asia, Southern Europe, and Arab cultures, for instance), it is relatively hard to challenge your manager, much less give loyalty to another boss where the relationship may not be as long-standing. In managing trade-offs and escalation in these cultures, individuals will normally give much more weight to their local manager. I have found this to be true throughout Europe, not just in the south.

European subsidiaries or divisions that I have worked with cling ferociously to local decision-making autonomy, even though their stance impacts standardization and overall quality.

Often a person working in a matrix from a remote location has to make decisions on priorities without direct input from their multiple managers. As a result, those issues that are of personal interest or have more discernable benefit receive more time. On the other hand, if a wider range of people involved in the matrix are equipped with the skills and tools to make intelligent trade-offs, the entire organization will benefit. This can be accomplished by opening lines of communication to include the full range of strategic and tactical goals, and by providing the necessary training so that personnel at remote locations can assume the responsibility for making choices where competing streams of activity have to be merged at the point where the matrix connects.

A recent example from my own experience points this out. While everyone in the worldwide organization I was working with understood the need for being cost conscious, each geographic division handled it differently. Despite the broader company goal for quality and unified management training, the senior managers in France who were in charge of management training for Europe decided that the priority was cost and contracted with less-expensive vendors locally. The result was a disconnect between the training received by European managers and their colleagues in North America with whom they frequently interact on projects.

I agree with Hall that the two major systems that exist to enable people to tell what is important to their businesses at any given moment are the budget system and the objective-setting and appraisal process. In many companies engaged in matrix management, these are still controlled centrally. The better solution is to measure, appraise, and finance people locally while encouraging them to think globally.

Before the introduction of matrix structures, most large companies had strong national country structures plus some kind of corporate staff function designed to integrate international operations. For corporate staff people, the matrix has probably made life easier, giving them more of a legitimate line role and aligning business activity at a supranational level. For these people, a more formal relationship, even if it is just a dotted line on the organization chart, has given more authority than when their only real tool was to influence the senior line manager in a country. For line managers, particularly the old country managers, the landscape has changed significantly. Before the matrix, they "owned" the country and the people based there. Now they have to negotiate resources, resolve trade-offs, and manage through influence and persuasion, without necessarily having traditional line authority.[7] Therein lies another potential problem for the matrix, since these country managers are not being trained with the new set of competencies and behaviors needed to negotiate the complexities and interpersonal dynamics of the matrix environment.

The country manager has been the main barrier to effective global matrix management. The matrix brings with it the perception that they are losing power. Working and getting things done through negotiating their way through a network of relationships demands a whole new set of skills, which appears contrary to the operational methods that have gotten them so far. In addition, these managers are faced with the challenges of managing teams that cross cultures, time zones, and available technology.

GLOBAL MATRIX ALARMS

There are some unmistakable signs that your global matrix isn't working. Here are some questions to ask that will point to the relative success of a working global matrix.

- Are several of your managers (and others) experiencing a high level of travel between the various outposts?
- Are some managers engaging in inappropriate micromanagement?
- Does there seem to be a lack of trust among the managers that their needs are being prioritized in a way that allows them to meet their objectives effectively?
- Are some managers demonstrating an overconcern about their visibility and how their job performance is being perceived?

The key to solving some of these problems is to build flexibility into the organizational culture. Flexibility is more important because global companies increasingly work with partners around the world. Leading companies effectively establish mergers, acquisitions, joint ventures, and strategic alliances vital in creating opportunities to combine capabilities and apply them across the global marketplace. They are at ease working through partnerships and networks of business relationships.[8]

Successful companies will engender a matrix mentality at all levels of management. The tendency to focus locally through strong but insular business units needs to be changed. To accomplish this, organizations need to build the capabilities required to operate globally. Managers and employees need to be trained to adopt the necessary behaviors to function in a flexible matrix organization.

- Working through varied and changing business relationships both internal and external to the parent organization.
- Developing a tolerance for ambiguity and complexity inherent in multidimensional matrix organizations.
- Applying negotiation and collaboration skills.
- Developing an understanding and respect for different cultures.
- Leveraging the strengths of diversity and working across borders.

- Placing emphasis on innovation and adaptability to rapid change.
- Integrating global and local perspectives in decisions and actions.

These capabilities are largely the same as those for all effective leaders with the added complexities of multiple cultures and multidimensional organizations. However, unless the organization is willing to invest in learning programs, rotating job assignments, and other activities that will develop these competencies, the resulting chaos and conflict will undermine the best efforts. Ironically, the failure of the enterprise will most likely be blamed on matrix management rather than the lack of necessary support to sustain and nurture it. Walker summarizes the issue this way:

Our challenge is to enable our managers and key employees to think and act both globally and locally. We must help our organizations develop capabilities (people, systems, resources) for worldwide advantage, manage the pitfalls and opportunities for cross-cultural management, and apply information and organizational systems for global knowledge sharing....We must build a workforce with the global business savvy, cross-cultural leadership skills, productivity, and capacity required to achieve results in the more complex global context.[9]

Globalization has forced companies to look at whether or not they are prepared to operate internationally or have a diverse workforce. Many companies that have never operated outside the United States are hiring foreign managers and outsourcing internationally. The functional style of management needs to adapt to incorporate teams located across the globe. Matrix management has the potential to support these new teams if it is implemented carefully and regulated throughout the project life cycle.

STRATEGIC ALLIANCES

While globalization is a major factor for external matrix management, the growth of strategic relationships as a way of doing business has accelerated in recent years. A strategic alliance is a mutually beneficial long-term formal relationship formed between two or more parties to pursue a set of agreed upon goals or to meet a critical business need while remaining independent organizations. It is a synergistic arrangement whereby two or more organizations agree to cooperate in the carrying out of a business activity where each brings different strengths and capabilities to the arrangement. The inception of a strategic alliance automatically creates a matrix because the combined set of dependencies is managed in varying degrees from two (or more) separate sources.

Strategic alliances potentially bring enterprises the following benefits:

- Increase in capital for research and product development and yet lower risk (innovation).

- Decrease in product lead times and life cycles (time pressures).
- Ability to bring together complementary skills and assets that neither company could easily develop on its own.
- Access to knowledge and expertise beyond company borders (technology transfer).
- Rapidly achieve scale, critical mass, and momentum (economies of scale; bigger is better).
- Expansion of channel and international market presence (enter a foreign market).
- Building credibility in the industry and brand awareness.
- Providing added value to customers.
- Establishing technological standards for the industry that will benefit the firm.[10]

Alliances range in scope from an informal business relationship based on a simple contract to a joint venture agreement in which for legal and tax purposes either a corporation or partnership is set up to manage the alliance. A strategic alliance is essentially a partnership in which you combine efforts in projects ranging from getting a better price for supplies by buying in bulk together to building a product together with each of you providing part of its production.

The goal of alliances is to minimize risk while maximizing the company's leverage and profit. An alliance is simply a business-to-business collaboration. Another term that is frequently used in conjunction with alliances is establishing a business network. Alliances are formed for joint marketing, joint sales or distribution, joint production, design collaboration, technology licensing, and research and development. Relationships can be vertical between a vendor and a customer or horizontal between vendors, local or global.

Larraine Segil (1996) in her book *Intelligent Business Alliances* sees alliances as the wave of the future in business and should be part of every organization's business plan. She points out that planning for an alliance is the key to success and provides some questions as guidelines.

- Why are we looking at an alliance now?
- What do we want to achieve from the alliance?
- Is an alliance the best way to achieve our goals?
- What resources are we willing to commit to this relationship?
- How is our company most comfortable in the creation of alliance relationships?
- How much control are we willing to cede to an alliance partner?[11]

These same questions could be guidelines for the development of a matrix strategy. Certainly, the last three questions point to core elements of matrix management.

The number of companies as well as not-for-profit organizations that could be used as examples of alliances and the matrix effect are exponential.

Some specialized examples with which I'm familiar include management consulting firms and high-level technology research. Consulting firms enter into short-term contracts or "engagements" with clients to produce positive change in the way the company does business. In most cases today, clients participate at a reasonably high level in the gathering of necessary data and the development of solutions. The results can be a new strategic direction, a more efficient and cost-effective supply chain, an operational improvement, or some combination of these objectives. Resource personnel from the consulting firm are generally housed at the client site, but retain sole membership as an employee of the consulting firm. This creates an interesting matrix because the client is the ultimate "boss," but does not control the resource. A natural tension develops as the host organization seeks to develop some control over the consultants.

One senior consulting executive describes the relationship as similar to a physiological event. The consultant enters the organization and is perceived as a threat (virus). The culture of the organization reacts to control or neutralize the threat (immune system). The success of an engagement is often dependent on the ability of both parties to negotiate the ensuing areas of conflict. "Scope creep," a common malady of consulting engagements, is a result of the failure to negotiate roles and a misalignment of expectations.

One consulting organization has built its entire business based on a matrix structure. Daymon Worldwide is a global company specializing in the sales and marketing of private-label consumer products. The company works with some of the leading retail, wholesale, and food service companies across the United States and in over a dozen countries, including supermarket and drug chains, mass merchandisers, warehouse clubs, specialty stores, food service, buying cooperatives, and wholesale distributors. Daymon has also built alliances with more than 3,500 manufacturers of all conceivable types of private-label products worldwide.

Daymon employs a concept of a retail "Service Package" that uses people, proprietary business systems, and customized sales and marketing programs designed to increase consumer awareness and sales and profits of corporate brands. Each "Service Package" is tailored to meet the specific and unique needs of the individual retail customer. Like other consulting firms, Daymon supports each of its customers with a specialized team. This team is located inside of, or in close proximity to, the customer's headquarters location. Depending on the needs of the customer, Daymon may offer many different services including business development and management, category analysis and management, and marketing management. The services include developing and managing relationships with the customer, manufacturers, and suppliers; taking on profit and loss responsibility for a business unit or a portfolio of product categories; and helping retailers market their private label to customers directly.

In one unique relationship, Daymon is working for a major retailer and is housed in its headquarters, but is compensated by the manufacturers and distributors who develop and provide the private-label products to the retailer. Complex networks of alliances such as this highlight the relationship side of making the matrix work. Unless the people involved have the ability and willingness to work together, the whole system will collapse under the weight of its own complication.

In order to operate successfully within the framework of global or alliance-focused organizations, emphasis must be placed on the relationship skills of the people charged with making these complex structures work. Through job experience and through education and development, we need to equip individuals to interact with people and build effective organizations in different national cultures as well as in different corporate cultures. We need to help them gain the sensitivity, flexibility, and knowledge required to work in diverse environments and to work effectively across the traditional borders of the organization. Effective performance with an extended matrix requires learning to share power; developing skills in listening, communicating, debating, and negotiating; and managing tensions and differences.

We need to build management processes and practices that work effectively in the complex business context, and continuously adapt them to changing requirements and feedback. Because of the need for flexibility and rapid change, the emphasis must be on product innovation, supply chain performance, and customer satisfaction. This means focusing on flexible roles, relationships, accountabilities, and competencies required to meet these ends.

The matrix helps organizations build a capacity to change rapidly and respond with targeted, effective organizational and business strategies. The key is providing the level of support necessary to manage the resulting complexity.

CHAPTER 10

Making the Matrix Work

> Theories of organization derive from the necessity of finding ways to coordinate technology, people, material resources, and the environment to compete effectively in the marketplace....There is no "best" theoretical approach to management practice. When something works well, it is because of a blending of the organization, the circumstances, the products, the personnel, the marketplace, and the personality characteristics of the individual manager.
>
> —Marvin Gottlieb[1]

In this concluding chapter, we will take a look at some of the factors that contribute to the successful implementation of a matrix organization. As part of the process, we will also look at several factors that work against this success. One interesting discovery for me has been that the same problems surrounding matrix management have endured for nearly thirty years. Davis and Lawrence (1978) examined the challenges of the matrix during the height of its popularity in the 1970s. They identified nine particular pathologies:

1. Tendencies toward anarchy—a formless state of confusion where people do not recognize a "boss" to whom they feel responsible.
2. Power struggles—managers jockey for power in many organizations, but a matrix design almost encourages them to do so.
3. Severe groupitis—the mistaken belief that matrix management is the same as group decision-making.
4. Collapse during economic crunch—when business declines, the matrix becomes the scapegoat for poor management and is discarded.

5. Excessive overhead—the fear of high costs associated with a matrix.

6. Sinking to lower levels—the matrix has some difficulty in staying alive at high levels of a corporation, and a corresponding tendency to sink to group and division levels where it thrives.

7. Uncontrolled layering—matrices which lie within matrices result frequently from the dynamics of power rather than from the logic of design.

8. Navel gazing—managers in a matrix can succumb to excessive internal preoccupation and lose touch with the marketplace.

9. Decision strangulation—too much democracy, not enough action.[2]

They suggest a number of preventive measures and remedies that also hold true for the matrix structures of today.

- Relationships between functional and product managers should be explicit so that people are in approximate agreement about who is to do what under various circumstances.

- Managers in a matrix should push for their advantages but never with the intention of eliminating those with whom they share power, and always with a perspective that encompasses both positions. They must see this sharing of power as an underlying principle, before and during all of the ensuing and inevitable power struggles. They always have to maintain an institutional point of view, seeing their struggles from a larger, shared perspective.

- Top managers need to accompany their strategic choice to move toward a matrix with a serious educational effort to clarify to all participants what a matrix is and what it is not.

- If managers start feeling emasculated by bilateral decision-making, they are certain to be unhappy in a matrix organization. In such cases, the strangulation is in the eye of the beholder. Such people must work on their personal decision-making style or look for employment in a non-matrix organization.

Davis and Lawrence conclude optimistically: "We believe that in the future matrix organizations will become almost commonplace and that managers will speak less of the difficulties and pathologies of the matrix than of its advantages and benefits."[3]

Unfortunately, the pitfalls identified by Davis and Lawrence outweighed the remedies they suggested. However, since the matrix is back, these remedies still apply. Hopefully, today's managers will have the foresight to pay heed.

The problem is that most organizations actively experimenting with the matrix—or being unwittingly engulfed by it—are not taking the necessary steps to ensure that managers and other personnel are properly prepared and trained to absorb the inevitable disruptions in the culture. These many years later, it is still rare to find a manager who understands the need to subvert their own need for authority and control to benefit the total organization. Even those managers who may have understood this when they were lower level employees fall into the same patterns of the managers they perceived as wrong on their way up. Even a bad model is irresistible when it's the only one you know.

USING THE MATRIX STRATEGICALLY

In a report titled "Structure Is Strategy: Gaining Strategic Advantage Through Organizational Design," Richard Kibble and Neal H. Kissel (2005) take issue with the "structure follows strategy" approach to organizational design.[4] They promote the notion that flexible structures produce flexible strategies. Although they do a good job of minimizing the use of the term "matrix" throughout the report, what they are describing is clearly a matrix approach to organizational design.

The report describes a top performing natural resources company that created a unique organizational structure that combines the advantages of small business units with "virtual structures" made up of groupings of business units that can address different strategic issues and competitive environments.

Each of the 100-plus business units represents a small team with accountability for strategy, resources and performance. This enables the CEO and his team to push accountability for value as close as possible to the "coal face," where value is actually created or destroyed. Moreover, there are no layers between these business units and the CEO and his team! The result: clear lines of sight for all managers.[5]

What is being described here is a highly tuned matrix organization, with accountability for both managing resources and creating value resting with the team. There is also some structured interaction between the teams in a "community" fashion discussed in an earlier chapter. Some business units have a collective accountability for managing the value of the company's relationship with a global customer group. Other business units have a similar collective accountability for a global supplier group or a strategy in a common geography.

These matrixed business units, called "virtual businesses" by Kibble and Kissel, have the ability to tackle corporate strategic issues that the functional business units can't address on their own without creating new layers of bureaucracy. "Moreover, because they are 'virtual,' these larger groupings of business units can be 'organized' in many different ways to meet the company's priorities, even as they evolve over time. This gives the company enormous capacity to organize and reorganize in response to an ever-moving agenda and competitive environment."[6]

By matrixing by geography, the company was able to organize four of its business units into a virtual business unit operating in a common region. This resulted in the identification and capture of $800 million of value creation. This was a direct result of having a better understanding than the competition of how the region's transportation economics could be dramatically improved by taking an enterprise-wide point of view across all operating units in the region. The competition could not see these opportunities because their organizational structures were defined by line of business, not region. Kibble and Kissel conclude that better global/local structures produce better global/local strategies.

The key to using organization design strategically appears to center around accountability. If the company is trying to serve both local and global markets at the same time without assigning accountability to both local and global business units, the competition may have a strategic edge.

One of the world's most profitable retailers addressed this challenge by creating both global category and local market business units, each with accountability for its end-to-end value creation. However, each business unit was also assigned specific "decision responsibilities" that relate to the decision factors it alone can execute to maximize end-to-end value of the overall business. This created a dramatically improved strategy, because the business units can react much faster to both local market and global category issues. For example, a price-based competitor in one local market was countered by selectively shifting certain key levers of pricing to local management. Strategic thrusts became more sophisticated as the company combined global category and local market intelligence. For example, a new premium range was launched only in prime central city sites instead of nationwide. Instead of focusing on revenues and costs that they alone can control, business unit management teams now focus on how to drive the end-to-end economics of the total business. This encourages a high level of global/local coordination without the need for coordinating bureaucracy.[7]

While it's hard to argue with success, the world's largest retailer, Wal-Mart, could potentially benefit from this strategy. On a recent search through a South Florida Wal-Mart for beach toys in January, I discovered that there were none available. It seems that Wal-Mart purchases everything seasonally, and the centralized purchasing authority allows no flexibility. So, because beach toys would languish on the shelves in Chicago, on a perfect beach day in Florida you can't buy a pail and a shovel.

REORGANIZATION AS A STRATEGY

One of the manifestations of today's matrix environment seems to be an epidemic of constant reorganization. Clearly, there needs to be some significant changes in the way the organization functions if matrix solutions are to be applied effectively. However, when change is not handled well, the result can be loss of jobs and loss of key people; demoralization of the workforce in general; increased worker turnover; decreased cooperation and teamwork; and increased levels of stress, anxiety, absenteeism, illness, and mistakes. These are not the attributes that contribute to a successful matrix implementation.

I have written elsewhere about the creation of a "Survivor" workforce that has developed a different type of relationship with their employers. Survivors are the people who are left when others are swept away. They were part of the company when the wave rolled in, and they are still part of the company when the wave carried others away. After the brow is mopped and the stomach has settled, after the good-byes to old comrades and some antagonists, what then? Forget and go on? Not likely. Picturing a man with his head in his hands and a confused, haunted look on his face, the August 4, 1986, issue of *Business Week* heralded "The End of Corporate Loyalty" on its cover.[8]

Amidst the general discussion of the erosion of loyalty (estimated as a 65% decline from ten years ago by a Business Week/Harris poll), the article discusses the survivors of cutbacks and suggests that survivors feel a sense of distance between themselves and the company. The individual begins to focus on personal security rather than corporate loyalty.[9] This would not seem to be a fertile ground to plant a new organizational strategy.

As early as fifteen years ago, a September 1992 article in the *National Business Employment Weekly* reported on a survey of thirty-one large companies by EnterChange, an outplacement firm based in Atlanta, GA. It indicated that restructuring programs designed to improve efficiency and profits had the opposite result—at least in the beginning. Employees' nonproductive time increased from 1.8 hours per day to 4.8 hours, while managers responsible for implementing the changes reported feeling lost. During the transitions, 59 percent of the companies' managers were perceived as not being effective in communicating a rationale to employees, 72 percent were unable to build a commitment to the new organization, and 77 percent didn't raise employee confidence levels. EnterChange double checked the data by interviewing 203 employees of a large organization undergoing a major change. According to the poll, 95 percent of employees reported having no specific job to perform during the transition. They also said they had difficulty completing their normal tasks because of distractions. Almost half said they had strong feelings of anger and bitterness, and 20 percent felt betrayed by the company. An estimate of company morale put it at 2.5 on a 10-point scale.[10] And yet, reorganization is not without its success stories. In their report, Kibble and Kissel (2005) describe the case of a CEO of a leading financial services company who has restructured his organization every eighteen months over the last five years and has achieved a 30 percent annual total shareholder return during the same period. They attribute the success to an ability to rapidly create new structures that provided a competitive advantage by placing organizational focus on the right issues at the right time across customers, products, and channels.

What they are describing is a mature matrix management organization at its best. A senior executive is completely accountable for the success of each business issue within the total organization. He or she is charged with delivering substantial value to the organization from resolving the issue. As soon as one issue is resolved, another emerges and the company's structure transforms to reflect the new set of priorities.

It's probably a safe bet that the ability to reorganize every eighteen months without creating a workforce nightmare didn't happen overnight. There is an evolutionary process that has to realign the people in such a way that they are receptive to this type of change. Kibble and Kissel do not provide a road map for getting to this fully realized matrix mechanism, but they do address the workforce issue at a high level.

There are two extremes in approaching the "people question" when building an organization. The first, "organize the staff:" design the organization to suit the talent you have. The other, "staff the organization:" find the best people to address the key challenges facing the organization. Our view is that you should organize around developing the talent you need in order to compete in the markets you serve.[11]

There are a lot of steps to climb before reaching that ideal. It is one thing to say, "We need to reorganize to be more effective than the competition." Then lay out a plan that looks right on paper but fails in the implementation because of the "built in" traditional and cultural resistance of the organization.

Let's look at another case that provides an interesting contrast. In 2002, Larry Bossidy and Ram Charan collaborated on a book titled *Execution: The Discipline of Getting Things Done*. A quote from Jack Welch trumpeted on the dust jacket, "A great practitioner and an insightful theorist join forces to write a compelling business story of 'how to get it done.'"

The book includes some examples of CEOs who, in their estimation, "got it done." One example provided discusses Dick Brown and his reorganization of EDS. In a nearly ecstatic review of Brown's performance at EDS, Bossidy and Charan (2002) talk about how Brown took a formerly troubled company in 1999 and embarked upon a bold plan to turn it around. No stranger to turnarounds, Brown had effectively returned Cable & Wireless, the British telecommunications giant, to profitability. As is so often the case, the same dynamic cited earlier in the case of Bosch & Lomb came into play. Brown and his consultant arrived at EDS with a solution and tried to fit the problem to it.

In the book, Charan demonstrates an understanding of the cultural issue but fails to address it at its fundamental level. Speaking of Brown, he says,

At EDS he faced a deeply embedded culture in need of fundamental change, one that was indecisive and lacking accountability, along with an organizational structure that no longer fit the needs of the marketplace.... Brown set goals for revenue and earnings growth so ambitious that most people in the company thought them impossible to meet. And he subjected the company to a massive reorganization.[12]

This is the classic "organizations have cultures" approach, and Brown believed that he could change EDS by fiat.

Bossidy and Charan paint Brown as the poster boy for execution. They consider bold moves as the means to make significant change in a relatively short time period. "Brown is deeply execution-oriented, and there was never any doubt who was in charge. While he points out that the transformation of EDS is still a work in progress, he successfully changed the fundamentals of the company in two years."[13]

Brown did make some correct moves with regard to the marketplace. He saw an opportunity to capitalize on the fast-growing new needs for information technology services. Keeping abreast of the changes in IT demands was a big challenge for even the best corporate IT department and a serious problem for companies with limited resources.

An examination of the core competencies of EDS seemed to indicate an ability to serve these markets. EDS could provide everything from routine operational services to strategic consulting at the highest levels through its consulting firm, A.T. Kearney, acquired in 1995. The company had a vast resource in technical expertise, and the experience in solving clients' problems provided a significant reserve of intellectual capital. Another positive was the can-do spirit embedded in the culture. This was a belief that EDS could do things for clients that seemed impossible. Working as a consultant for EDS, I learned that internally this can-do ethic is called the "Bob factor"— that in every case when called upon there is a mythical character named Bob who swoops in and does the impossible. This ethic endures to this day.

My interviews with current and past managers at EDS provide an interesting perception. Everyone agreed that something needed to be done. But the EDS structure consisted of nearly forty SBUs organized along industry lines, such as communications, consumer goods, and state health care. They divided the company into a confederation of fiefdoms, each with its own leaders, agenda, staffs, and sometimes policies. These fiefdoms rarely collaborated, and opportunities for new business were being lost. Most managers believed, as Brown did, that EDS would need a new organizational structure, along with significant changes in the culture. What was needed was more collaboration and accountability.

Many of his actions were arguably correct. He got to know the company by traveling around the globe for three months, meeting people at all levels formally and informally to talk and listen. He sent weekly e-mails to the whole organization, explaining his thinking and asking for feedback. He saw this approach as a tool to drive attitude change and encourage managers at lower levels to open their own dialogues with their direct reports. However, in a culture that was deeply embedded with the notion that communication was directive and not an open invitation for dialogue, Brown's actions were misinterpreted.

He began to disseminate information about company performance on a regular basis. For example, sales figures, which had formerly been compiled quarterly, were now reported daily, and for the first time the top 150 or so senior leaders were given the company's vital information, from profit margins to earnings per share. He instituted the monthly "performance call" that was supposed to encourage collaboration and accountability. Rather it was seen as controlling and punitive.

Bossidy and Charan, however, saw these calls as a positive step. "He, his COO, and his CFO began hosting Monday-morning conference calls of the company's roughly top 150 leaders. These calls are essentially an ongoing operating review, in which the company's performance for the previous month and the year to date is compared with the commitments people have made."[14] The calls were supposed to provide early warning of problems and instill a sense of urgency. People who fell short of expectations were expected to explain why and what they are going to do about it.

The idea was to bring a new reality to discussions of EDS operations. "The talks were supposed to focus on both the positive and the negative, and, to be fair, some of the senior executives saw these sessions as positive and constructive in intent. However, no one wanted to appear as doing poorly in front of peers. It amazes me that so many savvy people could mistake silence as agreement. Bossidy and Charan report that at one of the first meetings, one of the executives made the statement that he was worried about growing anxiety and unrest in his organization, worried about rapid and dramatic change. His people were asking, 'Are we moving too fast, are we on the threshold of being reckless? Maybe we should slow down, take it easy, reflect a bit.'"[15]

Brown, they report, turned the issue around and said, "I would like anybody on this call who is really worried about where we are going and worried about the fact that we will probably fail, tell me so right now. Don't be afraid to say you are. If you think we're making a big mistake and heading for the reef speak up now." No one did.

Brown's viewpoint was that if people in the organization were worried, it was the managers' fault. They were not doing a good enough job of communicating the company objectives down the line. At the same time, a large number of "under performing" executives were fired, a new compensation system that tied rewards to performance was developed, web-based evaluation tools were implemented to help line executives make better judgments about their personnel, and leadership development courses were planned for all levels.

Initially, Brown met his financial targets. The massive downsizing helped the bottom line and some of the marketing strategies paid off. However, the effects were not long lasting.

Although Bossidy and Charan avoid using the term "matrix management," a matrix was already in place at EDS. The forty-odd business units that were aligned according to the industry they served had little reason to collaborate. The observation that this matrix wasn't working was correct. EDS was a single-business firm trying to act like a multi-business firm. There were some centralized groups that provided services to the SBUs. However, the competition for these services was intense, as each industry unit was trying to customize everything that EDS had to offer for its customer. By rolling the

SBUs into a new organization of four lines of business centered on broad market segments, the matrix was simplified on paper, but did not change appreciably in fact.

E Solutions offered a complete range of services for the "extended enterprise." E Solutions linked electronically with suppliers and clients, from the supply chain networks to Internet security. Business Process Management provided businesses and governments with administrative and financial processing and client relationship management. Information solutions sold IT and communications outsourcing, managed storage, and management of desktop systems. A. T. Kearney was to specialize in high-end consulting, along with executive search service.

This new cut on the matrix divided the business according to markets and was supposed to allow EDS to fully leverage its intellectual capital for the first time, drawing on people from all parts of the company to provide solutions for clients. Collaboration among the lines of business would enable EDS to bring every client a value proposition based on its full "end-to-end" capability—from business strategy consulting to process redesign and management to Web hosting. The expectation was that the people from the old business units would learn not only their new jobs but also new ways of working together.

Bossidy and Charan conclude that the reorganization was a success. At the end of 2001, the company had achieved record revenues and solid market share gains, and chalked up eleven consecutive quarters of double-digit growth in operating margins and earnings per share. Its stock price was up some 6.5 percent from the time Brown took the job.[16]

The honeymoon was short. Roughly one year later, editorials like the following were appearing in the financial press.

Dick Brown Electronic Data Systems. What was he thinking? In August, well into the tech industry's season of discontent, Richard H. Brown, the 55-year-old CEO of Electronic Data Systems Corp. (EDS), told institutional investors and analysts that his company was faring better than its rivals: The Plano (Tex.) IT-services giant had plenty of deals in the pipeline that would assure big-time growth in the near future. He didn't say this just once, but over and over as he traveled around the country.

Six weeks later, on Sept. 18, Brown had to take it all back. Believe it or not, the recession had snuck up on EDS. Instead of growing, revenues would drop in the third and fourth quarters, and profits would sink by as much as 84%. It wasn't just the sluggish economy: The company had underestimated its costs on a few large contracts and had to take a $31 million charge. Investors sliced EDS's market value in half.

That wasn't the end of Brown's fiascos. Less than a week later, an analyst revealed that EDS had made an undisclosed $225 million payment to settle put options and purchase agreements on its own stock that had been entered into months earlier when shares were near their peak. Brown, who declined to comment, has said he has no plans to leave EDS. Sounds as if his optimism is getting the better of him again.[17]

So what happened? My interviews with EDS insiders who lived through those times provide some interesting insights. The prevailing feeling about the structure was that it didn't accomplish anything. Although the layers of bureaucracy were flattened from forty to around fifteen industry groups, any large customer had to deal with all four internal business organizations to get their needs met. Despite the simplification of the structure, the reality was that there were still industry groups and shared services groups. Because EDS was unable to customize everything, product decisions were being driven by larger customers.

In addition, based on encouragement and direction from Charan, with whom he had a long-standing relationship, Brown tried to develop a culture of "execution." Efforts were made to engage organizational leaders in the overall business success. Attempts were made to open lines of communication and make financial data more transparent. Managers were challenged to carry this message to the ranks. An elaborate system of intranet measures were put into place, and their use mandated. Yet, at the same time managers were being asked to be open about the difficulties they were experiencing with implementation of the plan, scores of their colleagues were being eliminated.

Later in their book, Bossidy and Charan refer to the strange isolation that some executives experience. "An astonishing number of strategies fail because leaders don't make a realistic assessment of whether the organization can execute the plan."[18] By becoming increasingly directive and placing so much emphasis on measurement of moment-to-moment performance, EDS leadership missed solving the fundamental issue: the people didn't know how to work effectively with each other. From my vantage point of working with both EDS and A.T. Kearney at the time, I can assert that the cultural divide between EDS and A.T. Kearney was as wide when Kearney and EDS parted ways in 2005 with a management buyout as it was when they were purchased in 1995. One former EDS executive put it this way: "Brown tried to create a culture of execution, but instead succeeded in creating a culture of compliance."

In 2004 under the leadership of Michael Jordan, who replaced fired chairman and CEO Dick Brown in March 2003, EDS began a dramatic turnaround. Jordan had led a major reorganization of Westinghouse Electric in the 1990s. He transformed the struggling industrial company by acquiring CBS, shedding its industry divisions, and turned the conglomerate into a pure media company under the CBS moniker. Jordan hung up his hat at CBS in 1998, but came out of retirement to revive EDS.

The turnaround artist didn't disappoint: EDS reported second-quarter net income of $104 million, compared to $26 million in 2005, and its $5.4 billion in contracts was up more than 100 percent over 2005's figure. In addition, the more than $15 billion in contract signings in first-half 2006 was the best six-month showing EDS has had since 2001. The results were aided on the outside by the creation of a new partnership known as the Agility

Alliance, a coalition of top technology firms led by EDS. But they were also brought on by successful partnerships internally, as the sales organization sought allies to effect changes in strategy and structure. Rather than simplifying the matrix, the concept was expanded to position the company to drive sales.

"People thought we were down and out. The hardest thing about that is [your employees start thinking], 'Are we gonna survive?'" says Michael Boustridge, EDS chief of sales and marketing. "You've got to tell your people, 'Stop, this is the path. But it's going to be tough. Transformation is tough.' Luckily, the sales organization had support from the top down."

"[Jordan] and the delivery heads are very supportive of sales," Boustridge says. "Everybody understands that it's everybody's job to sell." The department that would become sales' biggest ally, however, was human resources' Global Learning Development division, which helped develop a set of programs and processes to shape a new sales framework. "We very much had a successful partnership between two very disparate functions," he says.

The matrixing between functions seems to be working very well as part of the design. Perhaps the hardest part of the transformation, Boustridge says, was getting a global client-facing sales force, consistently between 2,000 and 2,500 people worldwide, to go from the transactional to the transformational sale. "[Before] we were probably having technology dialogues, but now we're having business dialogues," Boustridge says. In addition to training, taking a team approach to selling facilitates those dialogues. Now, it's common practice for account executives to bring subject-matter or delivery experts in on calls, while a back-office strategic sales center handles the processes that free up salespeople to get in front of clients. "You shouldn't have a meeting by yourself; you should always have someone there who has deep subject-matter expertise," he says. "The more people you can get talking to the client, typically the better the outcome."[19]

In addition to facilitating a working matrix internally, the process was extended externally. Central to Jordan's turnaround strategy was the creation of the Agility Alliance, in which EDS would work with major technology and business-services companies to create standardized solutions pieced together from the various partners' products. We have addressed the value of external alliances in a previous chapter, and for the moment, it appears that an extensive implementation of matrix management within a very short time frame has yielded major success for EDS.

One major difference between the current situation and the efforts that Brown made comes through in the attitude and enthusiasm of the managers interviewed in preparation for this book. Jordan has effectively engaged EDS's managers in a collaborative effort. They feel that they are valued members of a team rather than recipients of ongoing value judgments.

SUPPORTING INNOVATION WITH A MATRIX
THAT WORKS

Organizations cannot simply impose a structure that creates a flexible, customer-centered, competitive innovator. That approach has often led to serious negative consequences. The key to successfully responding to the market environment lies in the authenticity of a company's innovation culture. It must be more than a program, process, or initiative. It must be built into the organization at every level of the company. Done correctly, matrix structures provide great benefits. The company's ability to do what it says is greatly magnified.

Bartlett and Ghoshal (1990) articulate some of the fundamental strategic problems that companies continue to experience. Having moved from the simplistic solutions offered by consultants to avoid the complexity of changing environmental realities, and accepted the need to manage organizational and market complexity, many managers swung the pendulum toward matrix management. But, without the proper support and cultural background, the matrix proved unmanageable—especially in an international context. Dual reporting led to conflict and confusion; the proliferation of channels created informational logjams as a proliferation of committees and reports bogged down the organization; and overlapping responsibilities produced turf battles and a loss of accountability. Separated by barriers of distance, language, time, and culture, managers found it virtually impossible to clarify the confusion and resolve the conflicts.[20]

In a sense, the matrix became "deformalized" but didn't go away. As formal, hierarchical structure gives way to networks of personal relationships that work through informal, horizontal communication channels, the image of top management in an isolated corner office moving boxes and lines on an organization chart becomes increasingly anachronistic. This is from Bartlett and Ghoshal.

For those companies that adopted matrix structures, the problem was not in the way they defined the goal. They correctly recognized the need for a multi-dimensional organization to respond to growing external complexity. The problem was that they defined their organizational objectives in purely structural terms. Yet formal structure describes only the organization's basic anatomy. Companies must also concern themselves with organizational physiology—the systems and relationships that allow the lifeblood of information to flow through the organization. And they need to develop a healthy organizational psychology—the shared norms, values, and beliefs that shape the way individual managers think and act.

The companies that fell into the organizational trap assumed that changing their formal structure (anatomy) would force changes in interpersonal relationships and decision processes (physiology), which in turn would reshape the individual attitudes and actions of managers (psychology).[21]

Simply reconfiguring the formal structure without building up an appropriate set of employee attributes, competencies, and cultural perceptions will not bring success.

Every new initiative doesn't require reorganization or experimentation to create an innovative response. Workers at all levels are engaged, and pull together as a team rather than becoming entrenched as a survivor enclave. Functioning at its best, the matrix provides a sense of ownership in the improvement of how they work and what they produce. This is a sure formula for superior performance. Here are some guidelines for deploying a matrix structure that works.

Define a Strategy for Developing an Effective Matrix

1. There needs to be a conscious and sincere commitment to long-term change. This change needs the focus of all the leadership, but must be driven initially from the top.

2. Rethink the way employees work today. An obvious and understandable response to the competitive pressures of the global economy is to keep throwing more and more work at people. However, the research leads us to the conclusion that employers need to rethink the way employees work today. A useful analogy is competitive sports where it is well known that periods of recovery need to be interspersed within periods of "pushing hard."

3. For a matrix to work as a long-term strategy for the organization, corporate focus cannot be ephemeral. Often initiatives fail because the culture has a history of starting things that rapidly fade. Employees at every level need to see a consistent commitment in terms of money, process, and people devoted to the effort.

4. Successful matrix organizations nurture all of the various matrices in current operation, and learn from them.

5. The focus must begin with an understanding of the changing needs of the employees as well as of the external community (consumers, channel partners, suppliers, and vendors).

Develop the Infrastructure and Processes to Support the Matrix

6. Make serious efforts to create more effective workplaces. Such efforts should be based on empirical research that identifies critical aspects of an effective workplace. For example, employees who have jobs that provide them more opportunities to continue to learn, whose supervisors support them in succeeding on the job, who have the flexibility they need to manage their job and their personal and family life, and who have input into management decision-making are less likely to be change-resistant or feel overworked. This is true even when they work long hours and have very demanding jobs. Employers need to think about redesigning their workplaces to ensure that these and other critical components of an effective workplace are valued, worked toward, and part of the metrics for measuring success.

7. Determine what level of formal matrix your organization will support. If unsure, take an evolutionary approach and start with a balanced matrix. Work

out the kinks, and press forward toward a full matrix organization. Ask some questions:

- Where are the major problems? Distribution? Meeting customer demands for innovation?

- What are the other organizations in our category doing that appears to be effective?

- Think in terms of team integrity. Teams will work better if they are located in the same geographic area.

  Answers to these questions and others will help define the type of matrix structure that will work best for your organization.

8. Select and assign project managers who will each be responsible for a key segment or your product or service deliverables. These project managers must be provided with the authority for budget and staffing decisions, and made accountable for their deliverables. The project teams should be organized based on the needs of the deliverable rather than by functional department. Assuming that you don't have unlimited resources, this will create a climate of negotiation and trade-offs for personnel and other resources between the project managers and the functional managers. Because this is the major source of conflict in a matrix structure, special effort must be made to ensure that the lines of communication remain open and positive. Often, someone needs to take the role of facilitator. This can be a designated position (Matrix Manager) or someone from top leadership who has been assigned this role. A key element in managing potential conflict is the clear definition of roles and responsibilities. Create a policy statement and matrix document that clearly identifies project manager and functional manager responsibilities.

9. Facilitate collaboration between the project managers and the functional managers for several issues and potential flash points.

   - Staffing the teams should be a cooperative effort. Leverage the functional managers' insight into the skills and limitations of staff members.

   - Project managers must have significant input for performance appraisal. This should be supported by appropriate training and scheduled performance discussions between the project managers and the functional managers.

   - Clarification and re-clarification of reporting relationships need to be ongoing. Every effort needs to be made to remove as much ambiguity from the environment as possible.

10. Senior executives need to remain visibly involved. There needs to be ongoing support for the project manager authority and monitoring of the alignment between functional and program goals.

11. Put a great deal of thought and effort into the overall orientation to the changes.

    - The communication plan needs to be comprehensive and considerate of everyone's needs. Think in terms of the total organization.

    - Even if there are communities within the organization that will be minimally affected by the changes, they need to be kept informed.

    - Don't depend on written and/or electronic presentations. Conduct focus groups that allow all parties to participate and air their concerns.

- If internal expertise is not readily available, seek outside expert assistance in change management.

12. Develop or adopt tools and templates to track roles, responsibilities, timelines, and other factors that drive project success.

Bend the Culture to Embrace the Matrix

13. For a matrix to survive, it needs to be accepted in the organization's value system and culture.

- Identify those elements of the existing culture that actually support the broader objectives of the change. Use these as a springboard for launching a matrix or supporting an existing matrix.

- Keep lines of communication as open as possible. Seek the input of opinion leaders at all levels of the organization. Keep the doors open. Respond to all questions even if the answer is, "We don't know yet."

- Make it clear that there are important roles to be played by both project and functional staff members. Place the projected changes in the framework of opportunity.

- Keep the focus on the competition and how these changes will support a winning effort. Use language and other media to envision a prosperous future.

14. Invite and encourage collaboration whenever possible.

- Acknowledge and support all of the collaborative matrices already functioning in the organization. Examine and leverage those existing cross-functional relationships.

- Develop incentives and rewards for collaborative behavior. Again, if this is counterintuitive in the present culture, seek outside expertise.

- Develop a commitment to cultivating external relationships resulting in extended and expanded innovation resources and expertise (i.e., the not-invented-here syndrome has been removed from the equation).

Measure the Success of the Matrix

15. A comprehensive set of measures, rather than a single metric, better indicates the progress of change in the culture.

16. Measures specific to the business objectives at the program or department level enable timely and effective decision-making.

17. To ensure that the matrix initiative is not an island, measures for the amount of collaboration should link to measures of overall business performance.

DEVELOPING A MATRIX MANAGEMENT PHILOSOPHY

Some years ago on a pleasure and adventure trip with my family to Belize, we decided one morning to go to the zoo. Having been to zoos many times over the years, we had some assumptions about what we would find. Certainly, we expected some exotic animals like the tapir that are rarely seen in other places. We also expected an orderly arrangement of exhibits and habitats that provided a safe vantage point from where one can view the wild-life on display. In fact, the Belize zoo looked like a large area that had been enclosed by an unsubstantial wire fence sometime during the previous night to capture whatever animals happened to be there. Admittedly, this is an exaggeration, but not by much.

The highlight of the visit occurred when we saw a sign that said, "To the Crocodile." We walked down a dirt path until we came to another sign that said, "Prepare to Move Quickly!" Sure enough, around the next bend was a small muddy pond, and at its edge staring at us was the crocodile—without a fence!

The matrix management landscape is littered with the corpses of failed attempts to manage the complexity the structure brings with it. Despite a few examples to the contrary, simply laying out a matrix on an organizational chart often results in a brutal cultural war. Any new structure has the potential to create new and useful relationships, but these can take months and often years to evolve into effective knowledge-generating and decision-making engines for success. And since the new job requirements will frustrate, alienate, or simply overwhelm so many managers, changes in individual attitudes and behavior will likely take even longer.

The fact is that the matrix is here, and, barring any unforeseen cataclysmic change in the way the world is evolving, it's not going away. Organizations of every stripe need to examine it, assess its current effect on their way of working, and figure out what kind and level of support to provide in order to make it work better. In other words, the matrix needs to be embraced. It needs to have wire strung around it, organized and fed regardless of how it wandered in during the night.

The most successful managers of today have stopped trying to impose structural changes from the top down. Instead, they focus on the challenge of building up an appropriate set of employee attitudes and competencies and developing processes that support productive relationships both in and out of the organization. Indeed, the companies that are most successful at developing multidimensional organizations begin with cultural issues. Their first objective is to alter the organizational psychology—the broad corporate beliefs and norms that shape managers' perceptions and actions. Then, by enriching and clarifying communication and decision processes, they reinforce these psychological changes with improvements in the way the culture works. They act as if the organization *is* a culture rather than *has* a culture. When they have tied the necessary changes to the existing cultural norms in an acceptable way, serious organizational changes can take place in an acceptable and productive manner.

What is called for is a culture of collaboration. Corporate strategy has evolved through surviving several generations of painful transformation and has grown hybrids to manage the demands of the environment. Unfortunately, organizational development has not kept pace, and managerial attitudes lag even further behind. As a result, corporations now commonly design strategies that seem impossible to implement, for the simple reason that no one can effectively implement third-generation strategies through second-generation organizations run by first-generation managers.

Today the most successful companies are those where top executives recognize the need to manage the new environmental and competitive demands by focusing less on the quest for an ideal structure and more on developing the abilities, behavior, and performance of individual managers. Anyone with an eye toward building a matrix must begin with the fact that it's here to stay and probably is already functioning in the organization. The challenge is to build acceptance of the necessary collaborative behaviors within the culture in order to realize the greatest benefit of this flexible and powerful form.

In this book, I have tried to demystify and remove some of the demonizing effect that matrix management left in its wake twenty years ago. Most organizations will find that some level of matrix management will provide the flexibility and responsiveness to respond effectively in the ever increasing demands for innovation and change. The challenge is not so much to build a matrix structure as it is to create a matrix in the minds of our managers. The inbuilt conflict in a matrix structure pulls managers in several directions at once. Developing a matrix of flexible perspectives and relationships within each manager's mind, however, achieves an entirely different result. It lets individuals make the judgments and negotiate the trade-offs that drive the organization toward a shared strategic objective.

Appendix A

RASIC DIAGRAM

Many companies operating under the matrix style of management recently or after adopting it decades ago have never revisited whether or not it's working. In most cases, the original structure falls apart as people change jobs or companies are restructured or grow.

The matrix can be successful at implementing and coordinating cross-functional and multinational teams, but there needs to be tracking systems to make sure that everyone is on task. One system is called the RASIC, which is shorthand for Responsible, Approve, Support, Inform, and Consult.

	Person A	Person B	Person C	Person D	Person E
Task A	S	R	A	I	C
Task B	R	S	I	R	A
Task C	C	A	S	C	S
Task D	A	C	R	S	R
Task E	I	I	C	A	I

Each person on the team will have different roles regarding a task. Since each person on a matrix team comes from different parts of the organization, this is one way of listing all the roles for accountability.

Tools like RASIC cannot anticipate every scenario. Matrix teams that are organized in the beginning often fall into the habit of not revisiting the RASIC as a project progresses, yet the tool is intended to be dynamic.

When tasks or employees change, teams need to refer back to a chart like the RASIC to make sure they are on track and to update roles that have been completed. Without proper accountability measures, the matrix will not be effective. This type of responsibility matrix can group members of a team who are spread out internationally. Each person is aware of the other's role in the project and the sequence of tasks.

RCAI (OPTION)

The RCAI or Responsibility Chart is a variation of RASIC that can be more broadly applied to team issues outside of project management. This can be useful as teams are forming or as new work emerges as part of a team's responsibilities. A Responsibility Chart can be used to clarify understandings, improve the distribution of work, and build agreements that involve all and therefore can last.

A Responsibility Chart can be completed in several different ways:

- By the team as a group (this method may be somewhat time-consuming but will result in a high degree of commitment and understanding).
- By a subgroup of the team (this may be a bit more efficient. A review by the full team and agreement on the chart content would be an important second step).
- By each team member (the team would then need to confirm areas of agreement and discuss areas of difference to reach agreement).
- By the team leader (while probably the most efficient method in terms of time, discussion by the whole team is needed to ensure clear understanding and accountability).

SETTING UP THE RESPONSIBILITY CHART

The main parts of the chart are shown in the partial illustration below. These parts must be named to set up the chart for use. They are:

1. Place the *purpose* at the top of the chart. Defining exactly what project or work you want to understand is a vital first step in employing the chart.
2. Across the columns, list the people involved.
3. Next, list the tasks to be done. List these at the level of detail that seems right to you. You can increase or decrease that level as needed, and every task does not need be listed at the same level of detail. Look for the amount of detail that will ensure understanding and good distribution of responsibility.

SAMPLE RESPONSIBILITY CHART

	Person or Role			
	Administrative Assistant	Office Manager	CFO	Sales Manager
Task: Appreciation Dinner for Clients				
Create budget		I	I	R
Obtain approval for budget		C	A	R
Reserve room	R			A
Create guest list	R	A		C
Order invitations	R			I
Reserve caterer and plan food	R		I	A
Submit receipts	A	A	I	R
Reconcile accounts			I	R
Purchases <$500	A	C	I	R
Purchases >$500	A	C	I	R

Purpose: Responsibility Chart for determining distribution of financial responsibilities in the unit. Illustration (partially complete).

R, primarily responsible for ensuring task gets done; C, consults in planning and doing task; A, assists by doing some of the task; I, is informed of progress on task and when task is complete.

MAKING RESPONSIBILITY ASSIGNMENTS

Once you have completed the initial setup of the chart, assign letters in each of the boxes.

R—This person **is responsible** for carrying out the task, or accountable to see that the task is done. *Every task must have an R.*

Then assign letters A, C, and/or I as needed:

C—This person **consults** with the R person for the task. Consulting means that the two work collaboratively, with both having *significant responsibility* for doing the work.

A—This person **assists** the R person with the task. Assisting means this person helps carry out the work but is not as involved in making decisions about what is to be done or how.

I—This person **is informed** about the status of the work, including when it is done, but is not directly involved in planning or doing the work.

Appendix B

TEAM PERFORMANCE INVENTORY

Creating and maintaining productive teams require that some effort is put into examining the team process as well as the project issues. This inventory provides a way for the team to examine how things are going at various points in a project. The tool is a good springboard for discussion about how each member perceives the current health of the team and how it compares to the desired state of team health in the future.

METHODS FOR COMPLETING AND TALLYING THE TPI

1. The TPI (Team Performance Inventory) can be distributed and tallied by an outside facilitator. Responses are presented in the aggregate, without any individual's responses being revealed to the team. The facilitator can facilitate a team discussion on any or all of the questions.
2. Team members can complete the TPI with some members (or the team leader) tallying the response and facilitating the discussion. (This provides less anonymity than #1.)
3. Team members can complete the TPI and do the tally as a group. The team can then decide which items merit discussion.

WHAT ITEMS SHOULD BE DISCUSSED?

Items where the answers tend to "cluster" show areas where team members generally perceive team effectiveness on that scale in the same way. If team issues become apparent, the team can create some action plans to develop better skills or practices in the problem area that was identified.

Items where the answers are widely spread across the scale show a difference of perspective on the team. Team members may want to discuss how the team should best respond to the item in question. There needs to be consensus about the goals and agendas of the team.

Items with one or two answers very far from the others may indicate that one or two team members have very different perceptions of the team's effectiveness. Discussing and understanding the reasons for this difference of perspective can lead to a rich discussion; one goal for these conversations might be to address the unmet needs of team members with widely divergent perspectives.

TEAM PERFORMANCE INVENTORY

1. Team Goals

There is no consensus regarding team goals.　　　　　　　　　　There is consensus regarding team goals.

```
|-----------|-----------|-----------|-----------|
1           2           3           4           5
```
Comments: _____
_____

2. Member Contributions

Team members' contributions (information or ideas) are not recognized and/or utilized.　　　　Team members' contributions (information or ideas) are fully recognized and utilized.

```
|-----------|-----------|-----------|-----------|
1           2           3           4           5
```
Comments: _____
_____

3. Procedures

There is a lack of procedures to guide team functioning.　　　There are effective procedures to guide team functioning.

```
|-----------|-----------|-----------|-----------|
1           2           3           4           5
```
Comments: _____
_____

4. Imagination/Ingenuity

The team does not explore new ways of doing things.　　　The team is open to new methods and ways of doing things.

```
|-----------|-----------|-----------|-----------|
1           2           3           4           5
```
Comments: _____
_____

5. Assessment

The team never assesses its progress and productivity.　　　The team often assesses its progress and productivity.

```
|-----------|-----------|-----------|-----------|
1           2           3           4           5
```
Comments: _____
_____

6. Decision Making

There is no consensus as to how decisions are made.

The team has clear roles in how decisions are made.

```
|--------------|--------------|--------------|--------------|
1              2              3              4              5
```

Comments:

_____
_____
_____

7. Dialogue and Sharing

Team members do not share information amongst themselves or engage in open dialogue.

Team members openly share their experiences and expertise amongst the group and engage in open dialogue.

```
|--------------|--------------|--------------|--------------|
1              2              3              4              5
```

Comments:

_____
_____
_____

8. Diversity

Diversity and difference are not valued.

Diversity and difference are used and valued by the team.

```
|--------------|--------------|--------------|--------------|
1              2              3              4              5
```

Comments:

_____
_____
_____

9. Roles and Responsibilities

There is a lack of agreement on roles and responsibilities.

There are clear agreements on roles and responsibilities.

```
|--------------|--------------|--------------|--------------|
1              2              3              4              5
```

Comments:

_____
_____
_____

10. Resolve and Resolution

It is difficult for the team to resolve or come to a resolution about issues.

The team works collectively until a resolve or resolution emerges.

```
|--------------|--------------|--------------|--------------|
1              2              3              4              5
```

Comments:

_____
_____
_____

11. Appreciation and Value

I do not feel valued as an individual in the team. There is a lack of courtesy in how people treat each other within the team.

I feel valued as an individual member in team. There is a high level of respect and courtesy in how people treat each other.

```
|--------------|--------------|--------------|--------------|
1              2              3              4              5
```

Comments:

_____
_____

12. Interpersonal Communications

Communication within the team is closed and guarded.

There is open communication within the team.

```
|--------------|--------------|--------------|--------------|
1              2              3              4              5
```

Comments:

_____
_____
_____

13. Meeting Process

Meetings are not well organized
and lack focus.

Meetings are organized and
focused.

| 1 | 2 | 3 | 4 | 5 |

Comments:

_____

_____

_____

14. Meeting Outcomes

Meetings aren't productive. There
is little consensus and outcomes
are unclear.

Meetings are productive and
result in clear outcomes with
agreements summarized.

| 1 | 2 | 3 | 4 | 5 |

Comments:

_____

_____

_____

Notes

INTRODUCTION

1. Conrad, *Strategic Organizational Communication*, 23–31.
2. Ibid., 23.
3. Ibid., 25.
4. Mee, "Matrix Organization," 70–72.

CHAPTER 1

1. Anderson, "Matrix Redux—Matrix Management."
2. Mee, "Matrix Organization," 70–72.
3. Ibid.
4. Hunt, "Is Matrix Management a Recipe for Chaos?" 14.
5. Mee, "Matrix Organization," 72.
6. Ibid.
7. Anderson, "Matrix Redux—Matrix Management," 4.
8. Ibid.
9. Schrage, "A Jaded Look at Matrix Managements' Rebirth," 29.

CHAPTER 2

1. Editorial Staff, "US: GM Jobs Axe Now Poised over Salaried Staff," *Just-Auto.com*, March 28, 2006, http://www.just-auto.com/article.aspx?id=87209&lk=rap.
2. Schor, *Overworked American*.
3. Yankelovich, *New Rules: Searching for Self-Fulfillment*.
4. Ibid.

5. Galinsky and others, *Overwork in America*, http://www.familiesandwork.org/summary/overwork2005.pdf.

6. Tichy and Ulrich, "Leadership Challenge," 59.

7. Ibid., 62.

8. Ibid., 61.

9. Yankelovich and Immerwahr, *Putting the Work Ethic Back to Work.*

CHAPTER 3

1. Kolodny, "Evolution to a Matrix Organization," 543.

2. Ibid., 544.

3. Prahalad, "Strategic Choices in Diversified MNC's," 67–78.

4. Khandwalla, *The Design of Organizations*, 495.

5. Kolodny, "Evolution to a Matrix Organization," 544.

6. Massie, "Management Theory," 192.

7. Lawrence and Lorsch, *Organizations and Environment.*

8. "Grounds for a New Strategy," June 1.

9. Conrad, *Strategic Organizational Communication.*

10. Gottlieb, *Managing Group Process*, 56.

11. Sy and D'Annunzio, "Challenges and Strategies of Matrix Organization," 1–39.

CHAPTER 4

1. David A. Schmaltz, "Project Rituals," *Projects @ Work*, June 29, 2006, http://www.projectsatwork.com/content/articles/231864.cfm. Used with permission.

2. Overholt, "Flexible Organizations," 2.

3. Burns and Wholey, "Adoption and Abandonment of Matrix," 106–38.

4. Ibid., 109.

5. Ibid., 117.

6. Ibid., 133.

7. Levinson, "Zen and the Art of IT," 2.

8. Ibid., 3.

9. Ibid., 5.

10. Mehta and Vogelstein, "AOL: The Relaunch," 80.

11. Sherman, "Bausch and Lomb's Lost Opportunity," 105.

12. Ibid., 106.

13. Sy and D'Annunzio, "Challenges and Strategies of Matrix Organizations," 39–49.

14. Ibid., 5.

15. Ibid.

16. Ibid., 8.

PART II

1. Ashkenas, "Beyond the Fads," http://www.questia.com/PM.qst?a=o&d=5000290956.

CHAPTER 5

1. John Hunt, "Is Matrix Management a Recipe for Chaos?" *The Financial Times Limited*, January 12, 1998, 14.
2. Sayles, "Matrix Management: The Structure with a Future," 2–17.
3. Stuckenbruck, *Implementation of Project Management*, 85.
4. Ibid.
5. Kolodny, "Evolution to a Matrix Organization," 543–53.
6. FA News, "No Inflation Worries in TIPs Market," October 14, 2005, http://www.fa-mag.com/news.php?id_content=4~newsidnews=383.
7. Gottlieb, *Managing Group Process*, 75.
8. Gottlieb, *Getting Things Done in Today's Organization*, 15–17.

CHAPTER 6

1. Michael Tull, President, Tapestry Consulting, phone interview, May 29, 2007.
2. Grier, "Trait Approach to the Study," 316–23.
3. Gottlieb, *Managing Group Process*, 54–55.
4. Bormann, *Small Group Communication*, 205–14, 291–92.
5. Kenneth D. Benne and Paul Sheats, "Functional Roles of Group Members," *Journal of Social Issues*, Spring (1948): 42–47.

CHAPTER 7

1. Joseph Phillips, "Real World Project Management: Managing Your Human Resources," http://www.informit.com/articles/article.asp?p=391647&rl=1, June 3, 2005.
2. Nicholas, *Project Management for Business and Technology*.
3. Galbraith, "Matrix Organization Design," 29–41.
4. Grant, Graham, and Heberling, "Project Manager and Project Team Involvement," 1–8.
5. Dyer, "Partner Your Project."
6. Schmaltz, "The Good, Er, Old Days."
7. Schmaltz, "Someone Else's Goals."
8. Ibid.

CHAPTER 8

1. Abhay Padgaonkar, "Forest for the Trees," http://www.projectsatwork.com/content/articles/233756.cfm.
2. Baker, "Qualitative and Quantitative Analysis," 13–26.
3. McGregor, *Human Side of Enterprise*.
4. Fisher, "Leadership as Medium," 167–96.
5. Fiedler, *A Theory of Leadership Effectiveness*.
6. Blanchard and Zigarmi, *Leadership and the One-Minute Manager*.
7. Thomas and Kilmann, *Introduction to Conflict Management*.
8. Frank, *Persuasion and Healing*, 33.

9. Ibid.

10. Cialdini, *Influence: The Psychology of Persuasion*, 173.

11. Schrage, "A Jaded Look at Matrix Managements' Rebirth," 29.

CHAPTER 9

1. Thomas L. Friedman, "Anyone, Anything, Anywhere," *The New York Times*, September 22, 2006, New York Times Co., Reprinted with permission.

2. Treven, "Human Resource Management," 177–89.

3. "IBM Moves Procurement HQ to China," http://www.ibm.com/news/us/en/2006/10/2006_10_12.html.

4. Walker, "Are We Global Yet?" 8.

5. Hall, "International Matrix," www.global-integration.com/articles/12/international_matrix_management.html.

6. Ibid.

7. Ibid.

8. Walker, "Are We Global Yet?" 8.

9. Ibid.

10. "Strategic Alliance," *Wikipedia: The Free Encyclopedia*, http://en.wikipedia.org/w/index.php?title=Strategic_alliance&oldid=84770117.

11. Segil, *Intelligent Business Alliances*, 75.

CHAPTER 10

1. Gottlieb, *Managing the Workplace Survivors*, 53.

2. Davis and Lawrence, "Problems of a Matrix Organization," 131–39.

3. Ibid., 139.

4. Kibble and Kissel, "Structure Is Strategy," 1–10.

5. Ibid., 1.

6. Ibid., 2–3.

7. Ibid., 3–4.

8. Nussbaum, "The End of Corporate Loyalty," 42.

9. Gottlieb, *Managing the Workplace Survivor*, 6.

10. Capell, "Downsizing Doldrums," 16.

11. Kibble and Kissel, "Structure Is Strategy," 7.

12. Bossidy and Charan, *Execution: The Discipline of Getting Things Done*, 46.

13. Ibid.

14. Ibid., 48.

15. Ibid.

16. Ibid., 53–54.

17. Special Report, "The Best and Worst Managers," http://www.businessweek.com/magazine/content/05_02/b3915601.htm.

18. Bossidy and Charan, *Execution: The Discipline of Getting Things Done*, 195.

19. Julie Chang, "Team Player: EDS Partners for Profit,"*Sales, Marketing, and Management Magazine*, October 31, 2006, http://www.managesmarter.com/msg/content_display/sales/e3i2QoBjpYq8fh9hAxoSLfTCg%3D%3D.

20. Bartlett and Ghoshal, "Matrix Management," 139.

21. Ibid., 142.

Bibliography

BOOKS

Bormann, Ernest G. *Small Group Communication: Theory and Practice.* 3rd ed. Minneapolis, MN: Burgess International Group, 1996.

Bossidy, Larry, and Ram Charan. *Execution: The Discipline of Getting Things Done.* New York: Crown Business, 2002.

Cialdini, Robert B. *The Psychology of Persuasion.* Rev. ed. New York: Quill, William Morrow, 1993.

Conrad, Charles. *Strategic Organizational Communication: Towards the Twenty-First Century.* 3rd ed. Fort Worth, TX: Harcourt Brace, 1994.

Fiedler, Fred E. *A Theory of Leadership Effectiveness.* New York: McGraw Hill, 1967.

Frank, Jerome D. *Persuasion and Healing: A Comparative Study of Psychotherapy.* New York: Schoken Books, 1961.

Gottlieb, Marvin. *Getting Things Done in Today's Organization: The Influencing Executive.* Westport, CT: Quorum Books, 1999.

———. *Managing Group Process.* Westport, CT: Praeger Publishers, 2003.

———. *Managing the Workplace Survivors: Organizational Downsizing and the Commitment Gap*, 53. Westport, CT: Quorum Books, 1995.

Khandwalla, Pradip N. *The Design of Organizations.* New York: Harcourt Brace Janovic, 1977.

Lawrence, Paul, and Jay Lorsch. *Organizations and Environment.* Boston: Harvard Business School, 1967.

Massie, J.L. "Management Theory." In *Handbook of Organizations.* Edited by J.G. March. Chicago: Rand McNally, 1965, 192

McGregor, Douglas. *The Human Side of Enterprise.* New York: McGraw Hill, 1960.

Nicholas, J.M. *Project Management for Business and Technology.* 2nd ed. Upper Saddle River, NJ: Prentice Hall, 2001.

Schor, Juliet. *The Overworked American: The Unexpected Decline of Leisure.* New York: Basic Books, HarperCollins Publishers, Inc., 1993.

Segil, Larraine. *Intelligent Business Alliances.* New York: New York Times Books, 1996.
Stuckenbruck, Linn. *The Implementation of Project Management: The Professional's Handbook.* Reading, MA: Addison Wesley, 1981.
Thomas, Kenneth W., and Ralph H. Kilmann. *Introduction to Conflict Management.* Mountain View, CA: CCP, Inc., 1974.
Yankelovich, Daniel. *New Rules: Searching for Self-Fulfillment in a World Turned Upside Down.* New York: Bantam Books, 1982.
Yankelovich, Daniel, and John Immerwahr. *Putting the Work Ethic Back to Work: A Public Agenda Report on Restoring America's Competitive Vitality.* Dubuque, IA: The Public Agenda Foundation, 1983.
Zigarmi, Patricia, and Ken Blanchard. *Leadership and the One-Minute Manager: Increasing Effectiveness Through Situational Leadership.* New York: William Morrow and Company, 1985.

ARTICLES

Anderson, Richard E. "Matrix-Redux—Matrix Management." *Business Horizons* 11–12 (1994): 4.
Ashkenas, Ronald N. "Beyond the Fads: How Leaders Drive Change with Results." *Human Resource Planning* 17, no. 2 (1994). http://www.questia.com.
Baker, Deborah C. "A Qualitative and Quantitative Analysis of Verbal Style and the Elimination of Potential Leaders in Small Groups." *Communication Quarterly* 39, Winter (1990): 13–26.
Bartlett, Christopher A., and Sumatra Ghoshal. "Matrix Management: Not a Structure, a Frame of Mind." *Harvard Business Review* July–August (1990): 139.
Brache, Alan. "USA Today." *Society for the Advancement of Education,* May, 2001.
Burns, Lawton R., and Douglas Wholey, "Adoption and Abandonment of Matrix Management Programs: Effects of Organizational Characteristics and Inter-Organizational Networks," *Academy of Management Journal* 36 (1993): 58–76.
Capell, Perri. "Downsizing Doldrums." *National Business Employment Weekly* September 18–24 (1992): 16.
Davis, Stanley, and Paul R. Lawrence. "Problems of a Matrix Organization." *Harvard Business Review* 68 (1978): 131–39.
Dyer, Sue. "Partner Your Project." *Projects at Work,* July 13, 2006.
Editorial Staff. "US: GM Jobs Axe Now Poised over Salaried Staff." *Just-Auto.com,* March 28, 2006. http://www.just-auto.com.
Fisher, B. Aubrey. "Leadership as Medium: Treating Complexity in Group Communication Research." *Small Group Behavior* 16 (1985): 167–96.
Friedman, Thomas L. "Anyone, Anything, Anywhere." *New York Times,* September 22, 2006. http://select.nytimes.com.
Galbraith, J.R. "Matrix Organization Design." *Business Horizons* 14, no. 1 (1971): 29–41.
Grant, Kevin P., Scott T. Graham, and Michael E. Heberling. "The Project Manager and Project Team Involvement: Implications for Project Leadership." *Journal of Leadership Studies* 7 (2001): 106–19.
Grier, John C. "A Trait Approach to the Study of Leadership in Small Groups." *Journal of Communication* 17 (1967): 316–23.
"Grounds for a New Strategy—Coffee Industry Needs a Boost." *American Demographics,* June 1, 2001.

Hall, Kevan. "International Matrix." *Worldlink Newsletter*, January 2001. http://www.globalintegration.com.

Hunt, John W., "Is Matrix Management a Recipe for Chaos?" *Financial Times*, January 12, 1998.

Kibble, Richard, and Neal H. Kissel. "Structure Is Strategy: Gaining Strategic Advantage Through Organizational Design." *Marakon Commentary* V, no. 4 (2005): 1–10.

Kolodny, Harvey F. "Evolution to a Matrix Organization." *Academy of Management Review* 4, no. 4 (1979): 543.

Levinson, Meredith. "Zen and the Art of IT Governance." *CIO Magazine*, February 15 (2000): 2.

Mee, John. "Matrix Organization." *Business Horizons* Summer (1964): 70–72.

Mehta, Stephanie N., and Fred Vogelstein. "AOL: The Relaunch." *Fortune* 152, no. 10 (2005): 78–82.

Nussbaum, Bruce. "The End of Corporate Loyalty." *Business Week*, August 4 (1986): 42.

Overholt, Miles H. "Flexible Organizations: Using Organizational Design as a Competitive Advantage."*Human Resource Planning* 20, no. 1 (1997): 2.

Padgaonkar, Abhay. "Forest for the Trees." *Projects at Work*, November 2, 2006. http://www.projectsatwork.com.

Prahalad, C.K. "Strategic Choices in Diversified MNCs." *Harvard Business Review* 54, no. 4 (1976): 67–78.

Sayles, Leonard. "Matrix Management: The Structure with a Future." *Organizational Dynamics* 7 (1976): 2–17.

Schmaltz, David. "Project Rituals." *Projects at Work*, June 29, 2006. http://www.projectsatwork.com.

———. "Someone Else's Goals." *Projects at Work*, May 15, 2006. http://www.projectsatwork.com.

———. "The Good, Er, Old Days." *Projects at Work*, April 27, 2006. http://www.projectsatwork.com.

Schrage, Michael. "A Jaded Look at Matrix Managements' Rebirth." *Computer World* July 13 (1998): 29.

Sherman, Stratford P. "Bausch and Lomb's Lost Opportunity." *Fortune* 107 (1983): 105.

Special Report. "The Best and Worst Managers." *Business Week*, January 13, 2003. http://www.businessweek.com.

Sy, Thomas, and Laura Sue D'Annunzio. "Challenges and Strategies of Matrix Organization: Top Level and Mid Level Managers' Perspectives." *HR Human Resources Planning* 28, no. 1 (2001): 1–39.

———. "Problems of a Matrix Organization." *Harvard Business Review* 68 (1979): 131–39.

Tichy, Noel M., and David O. Ulrich. "The Leadership Challenge—A Call for the Transformational Leader." *Sloan Management Review* Fall (1984): 59.

Treven, Sonja. "Human Resource Management in International Organizations." *Management* 6 (2001): 177–89.

Walker, James W. "Are We Global Yet." *Human Resource Planning* 21, no. 24 (1998): 8.

WEB SITES

FA News. "No Inflation Worries in TIPs Market." October 14, 2005. http://www.fa-mag.com/news.php?id_content=4~newsidnews=383.

Galinsky, Ellen, James T. Bond, Stacy S. Kim, Lois Backon, Erin Brownfield, and Kelly Sakai. "Overwork in America: When the Way We Work Becomes Too Much." Families and Work Institute. http://www.familiesandwork.org/summary.overwork2005.pdf.

"IBM Moves Procurement HQ to China." http://www.ibm.com/news/us/en/2006/10/2006_10_12.html.

"Strategic Alliance." *Wikipedia: The Free Encyclopedia.* http://www.wikipedia.org.

Index

About the Author

MARVIN R. GOTTLIEB is President of The Communication Project, Inc., a management consulting and training firm through which he provides executive coaching and career development to senior managers in a wide variety of organizations. Previously, he held the position of Associate Professor of Communications at Lehman College-CUNY, where he taught courses in organizational communication and group dynamics. A popular speaker at industry conferences, he is the author of several books, including *Managing the Workplace Survivors* (Quorum, 1995), *Getting Things Done in Today's Organization* (Quorum, 1999), and *Managing Group Process* (Praeger, 2003).

CPSIA information can be obtained at www.ICGtesting.com
Printed in the USA
LVOW072221200312

274050LV00007B/10/P